HOW WE UNDERSTAND THE WORLD
How To Study the World

ALAN MACFARLANE was born in Shillong, India, in 1941 and educated at the Dragon School, Sedbergh School, Oxford and London Universities. He is the author of over twenty published books, including The Origins of English Individualism (1978) and Letters to Lily: On How the World Works (2005). He has worked in England, Nepal, Japan and China as both an historian and anthropologist.

He was elected to the British Academy in 1986 and is now Emeritus Professor of Anthropology at the University of Cambridge and a Life Fellow of King's College, Cambridge.

How To Study The World
Suggestions for Shuo

ALAN MACFARLANE

2018

CAM RIVERS PUBLISHING

First published in Great Britain in 2018

5 Canterbury Close
Cambridge CB4 3QQ

www.cambridgerivers.com
press@cambridgerivers.com

Author: Alan Macfarlane
Series Editor: Zilan Wang
Editor: Sarah Harrison
Marketing Manager: James O'Sullivan
Typesetting and cover design: Jaimie Norman

The publication of this book has been supported by
the Kaifeng Foundation.

© Alan Macfarlane, 2018

The moral right of the author
has been asserted.

All rights reserved. Without limiting the rights under copyright reserved above, no part of this publication may be reproduced, stored or introduced into a retrieval system, or transmitted, in any form or by any means (electronic, mechanical, photocopying, recording or otherwise), without prior written permission of both the copyright owner and publisher of this book.

For Shuo, with my love.
Alan Macfarlane, 2017

Contents

PREFACE: *The Missing Manual*		9
	ENCOUNTER WITH THE WORLD	13
1	Reading and Connecting	14
2	Conversations	15
3	Experience: Participating and Observing	37
	RE-IMAGINING THE WORLD	55
4	Imagining	56
5	Writing	65
	EXPLAINING THE WORLD	76
6	Frameworks of Understanding and Explanation	77
7	Time and Space	85
8	Contrast and Comparison	96
AFTERWORD		106
Further Reading and References		108

PREFACE

The Missing Manual

Dear Shuo,

All humans try to understand their world in order to survive and thrive. I have been fortunate to have lived a long life in which my job as a University teacher has allowed me to turn this necessity into the way I earn my living. Through a training at school and then in four degrees in history and anthropology, followed by nearly forty years of teaching, researching and writing at Cambridge University, I have tried to understand different worlds, past and present, in Europe and Asia.

I learnt some of the methods for doing this as an undergraduate and in three postgraduate degrees, but discovered later that very few of the practical techniques – how to write, how to index, how to use comparison and contrast – were explicitly taught to me, even in the best universities in the world. Instead, I have learnt almost all I know about such methods from watching, reading and talking to people who seem to have been particularly creative and who have penetrated deeply into the complexities of past and present worlds. From this knowledge I tried to pass on my experience to my students over the generations, having discovered what worked best in my own life.

This short book, written for my friends and students, past and future, will deal as simply as I can with some of the ways in which we can make our encounter with diverse worlds more fruitful.

Each reader will have to adapt and select from what I say. Yet it may be that out of a lifetime of distilled experience of being involved in many historical and anthropological projects, teaching numerous very clever students, lecturing to many different audiences, and writing over eighty books (half of them published in one form or another), something helpful can be found by a new generation.

The book is one in a set of books primarily written for an audience of young people trying to understand their world. It started with *Letters to Lily: On How the World Works* (2005) and subsequently there have been other books with titles such as *How Do We Know*, *How To Discover the World*, *How To Investigate Mysteries*, which complement this work. So there are a set of inter-linked fruits of my wider attempt to study what I call 'The Riddle of the Modern World.'

The book follows Einstein's advice to 'Make Things as Simple as Possible – but not Simpler.' It is explicitly influenced by Marc Bloch's wonderfully clear and simple synthesis of his life as a historian, *The Historian's Craft* (1954), which was written in a German prisoner of war camp before he was shot. The set of books are thus my attempt to follow René Descartes in his brief and simple *Discourse on Method* (1637), where he lays out the basic methods of the physical sciences. Here I am trying to do the same for the humanities and social sciences.

* * *

I shall divide the complex process of trying to understand our world into three parts. In the first I discuss three of the major ways in which we learn about our world – through participation, conversation and absorbing creative works by writers and artists.

I will then look at how this experience is worked upon, reshaped and communicated both to ourselves and others through our imagination and through creating a piece of writing. Finally I shall broaden out into a more philosophical section about the way in which the questions we ask and the answers which we are prepared to accept are shaped by the wider cultural context in which we live, including our frame of comparison.

Encounter with the World

I HAVE LEARNT about how the world works through my education and travels in three main ways. The first major source of knowledge is to look at or read what others have found out and represented in their poetry, novels, academic books, films and plays. Nowadays, in particular, we learn most of what we know from visual media, but writing continues to be important as a form of condensed information. I have a large library and have studied the works of many great predecessors who have tried to understand the world. Their insights have shaped my understanding, so I shall discuss reading and in particular how the reading can be turned into a more active and creative activity through working over what we discover through a system of indexing and dynamic note-taking.

The second way I have learnt about the world is through talking to people. From the extreme of fragmentary conversation, through to very carefully planned and structured interviews, we test out our ideas and try to enter the mind and emotional worlds of others. So I have learnt most of what I know about my own society, as well as others I have spent a long time in – Nepal, Japan and China – from such conversations. I have made the film interviewing of interesting thinkers a central project in my attempt to try to understand the world.

The third and most important is through experience, or what, when formalized by the social sciences, came to be known as the method of 'participant-observation.' We are all participant-observers from our birth, of course, but it is a method we can use more explicitly to try to understand ourselves and other societies. So I will describe something of what I have learnt about the method through using it in many contexts, in particular in twenty periods of fieldwork over a period of nearly fifty years in the Himalayas.

ONE

Reading and Connecting

WE 'READ' BOOKS, films, plays and other people, turning signs and symbols whether on a television screen, in a newspaper or another's face into something which we think we can understand. The process is immensely complex and most of us spend many years being taught how to 'read' various media, especially written forms. We may come across people who give us good advice about the process. For example, that different media are read in different ways; that some books should be read carefully, others skimmed, others dipped into; that we should think seriously before we read about what it is we are looking for. So we do get some instruction on 'reading.'

What is much less well taught is how we then process what we 'read' so that we can use it through the years as we try to understand the world. This has been a hobby of mine since I was a child, so it I will outline what I have learnt about the second stage of 'reading,' namely storing and re-creating the materials into a new shape. Let me start with some general thoughts on the way we think creatively.

* * *

There are ample indications that those who have most enriched our view of the world have done this through making curious and unexpected connections based on reading and reflection. Writing of Max Weber, for instance, Collins states: 'He is full of unexpected insights and subterranean connections, although many of them have proved too forbidding for most readers attempting to dig through the unaccustomed historical examples...'[1] The external manifestations of this process are described by Alexis de Tocqueville: 'When I have gathered in this toilsome harvest, I retire, as it were, into myself; I examine with extreme care, collate and connect the notions which I have acquired, and I make it a rule to give the result, without bestowing a thought on the inferences which others may draw from what I write.'[2]

How does the mind think it is working in these moments of inspiration? A few classic accounts are worth citing. One is by the geneticist Galton. 'There seems to be a presence-chamber in my mind where full consciousness holds court, and where two or three sides are at the same time in audience, and an antechamber full of more or less allied ideas, which is situated just beyond the full ken of consciousness. Out of this ante-chamber the ideas most nearly allied to those in the presence-chamber appear to be summoned in a mechanically logical way, and to have their turn of audience.'[3] This is one of the most powerful metaphors for that groping on the edges of consciousness which seems always to be present in great science and art.

Another hint of the process, with a similar idea of a core and margins, is given by the psychologist William James. 'The great

---

1 COLLINS, RANDALL, *Weberian Sociological Theory* (1986), p.7.
2 DE TOCQUEVILLE, ALEXIS., *Memoir, Letters, and Remains of Alexis de Tocqueville* (1861), p.2,339.
3 FRANCIS GALTON quoted in KOESTLER, ARTHUR, *The Act of Creation* (1964), p.160

field for new discoveries is always the unclassified residuum. Round about the accredited and orderly facts of every science there ever flows a sort of dust-cloud of exceptional observations, of occurrences minute and irregular and seldom met with, which it always proves more easy to ignore than to attend to.'[1]

The need to connect is further described by the great French mathematician Henri Poincaré in a famous analysis. 'Among chosen combinations the most fertile will often be those formed of elements drawn from domains which are far apart... Most combinations so formed would be entirely sterile; but certain among them, very rare, are the most fruitful of all.'[2]

This passage looks similar to, but is not identical to, another valuable piece by Poincaré in Nadel, which is also worth quoting: 'The experimental method is intended to 'reveal unsuspected relations between.... facts, long since known, but wrongly believed to be unrelated to each other. Among the combinations we choose, the most fruitful are often those which are formed of elements borrowed from widely separated domains.'[3]

The combinations occur from shaking and juxtaposing. "It is obvious", says Hadamard, "that invention or discovery, be it in mathematics or anywhere else, takes place by combining ideas...the Latin verb 'cogito' for 'to think' etymologically means 'to shake together.' St. Augustine had already noticed that and also observed that 'intelligo' means 'to select among.'"[4]

Koestler's own observations on the creative process are worth noting. Creativity '...is signalled by the spontaneou flash of insight which shows a familiar situation or event in a new light,

---

[1] WILLIAM JAMES quoted in KOESTLER, *Creation*, p.191.
[2] KOESTLER, *Creation*, p.164.
[3] POINCARE quoted in NADEL, S.F., *The Foundations of Social Anthropology* (1963)
[4] HADAMARD quoted in KOESTLER, *Creation*, p.191.

and elicits a new response to it. The bisociative act connects previously unconnected matrices of experience; it makes us "understand what it is to be awake, to be living on several planes at once" (to quote T.S. Eliot, somewhat out of context).[1] This process 'does not create something out of nothing; it uncovers, selects, re-shuffles, combines, synthesizes already existing facts, ideas, faculties, skills.'[2]

There is a 'sudden interlocking of two previously unrelated skills, or matrices of thought.'[3] Or, to put it another way, 'All decisive advances in the history of scientific thought can be described in terms of mental cross-fertilization between different disciplines.'[4] We begin to see similarities where before there was only difference. 'The most important feature of original experimental thinking is the discovery of overlap and agreement where formerly only isolation and difference were recognized.'[5]

How does one achieve this? One element is the necessity to forget. It is important to be able to forget what we already think we know. 'To undo wrong connections, faulty integrations, is half the game. To acquire a new habit is easy, because one main function of the nervous system is to act as a habit-forming machine; to break out of the habit is an almost heroic feat of mind or character. The prerequisite of originality is the art of forgetting, at the proper moment, what we know.'[6]

Another element is the placing of our material in another context: '...the art of handling the same bundle of data as before, but placing them in a new system of relations with one

---

1 KOESTLER, *Creation*, p.45
2 KOESTLER, *Creation*, p.120
3 KOESTLER, *Creation*, p.121
4 KOESTLER, *Creation*, p.230
5 KOESTLER, *Creation*, p.232
6 KOESTLER, *Creation*, p.190

another by giving them a different framework, all of which virtually means putting on a different kind of thinking-cap for the moment.'[1] One way of achieving this is to force ourselves into new challenges. 'But to recapture the erstwhile magic in all its freshness, he must turn to something new; experimental theatre, avant-garde films, or Japanese Kabuki, perhaps; novel experiences which compel him to strain his imagination, in order to make sense of the seemingly absurd - to participate, and re-create.'[2]

There may be even more practical advice. Darwin had his 'thinking path' along which he would stride, trying to sort out his ideas. In this he was demonstrating Max Weber's view that: "Both, enthusiasm and work, and above all both of them jointly, can entice the idea. Ideas occur to us when they please, not when it pleases us. The best ideas do indeed occur to one's mind in the way in which Ihering describes it: when smoking a cigar on the sofa; or as Helmholtz states of himself with scientific exactitude: when taking a walk on a slowly ascending street; or in a similar way. In any case, ideas come when we do not expect them, and not when we are brooding and searching at our desks. Yet ideas would certainly not come to mind had we not brooded at our desks and searched for answers with passionate devotion."[3]

'ONE FACT ONE CARD'

One classic account of the method which can liberate the

---

[1] KOESTLER, *Creation*, p.235
[2] KOESTLER, *Creation*, p.336
[3] GERTH, H.H & MILLS C. WRIGHT (eds.), From *Max Weber: Essays in Sociology* (1967), p.136.

material we encounter from its original context and allow the mind to re-arrange it, is described by Beatrice Webb.

In the appendix to *My Apprenticeship*, Beatrice Webb wrote: 'It is difficult to persuade the accomplished graduate of Oxford or Cambridge that an indispensable instrument in the technique of sociological enquiry – seeing that without it any of the methods of acquiring facts can seldom be used effectively – is the making of notes.'[1]

The method of writing 'one fact on one card' which she described 'enables the scientific worker to break up his subject-matter, so as to isolate and examine at his leisure its various component parts, and to recombine them in new and experimental groupings in order to discover which sequences of events have a causal significance.'[2]

The liberating effects of this shuffling of paper are well described. 'To put it paradoxically, by exercising your reason on the separate facts displayed, in an appropriate way, on hundreds, perhaps thousands, of separate pieces of paper, you may discover which of a series of hypotheses best explains the processes underlying the rise, growth, change or decay of a given social institution, or the character of the actions and reactions of different elements of a given social environment.'[3]

Physical details are important. For instance, a standardized size of card, and placing the same information in the same place on the card, makes it easier to move quickly through the materials. 'Thus, a carefully planned "display", and, above all, identity of arrangement, greatly facilitates the shuffling

---

[1] WEBB, BEATRICE, *My Apprenticeship* (1st *edn.*), pp.426-7
[2] WEBB, *Apprenticeship*, p.427.
[3] WEBB, *Apprenticeship*, p.427.

and reshuffling of the sheets, according as it is desired to bring the facts under review in an arrangement according to place, time or any other grouping.'[1] For instance, 'By adopting our method of one sheet for one subject, one place and one date, all the sheets could be rapidly reshuffled in chronological order; and the whole of our material might have been surveyed and summarised exclusively from the standpoint of chronology.'[2]

The result of this mechanical device was that it was possible to look at questions in numerous different ways: 'By the method of note-taking that I have described, it was practicable to sort out all our thousands of separate pieces of paper according to any, or successively according to all, of these categories or com-bination of categories...'[3] It also, most importantly, provoked clashes and surprises. 'Not once, but frequently has the general impression with regard to the causal sequence of events, with which we had started our enquiry, or which had arisen spon-taneously during the examination of documents, the taking of evidence or the observation of the working of an organisation, been seriously modified, or completely reversed, when we have been simultaneously confronted by all the separate notes relating to the point at issue.[4] Beatrice Webb again notes the surprising effects on creativity of this apparently simple strategy. 'I realise how difficult it is to convince students – especially those with a 'literary' rather than a 'scientific' training – that it is by just this use of such a mechanical device as the shuffling of sheets of notes, and just at this stage, that the process of investigation is often fertile in

---

1   WEBB, *Apprenticeship*, p.340.
2   WEBB, *Apprenticeship*, p.432.
3   WEBB, *Apprenticeship*, p.432.
4   WEBB, *Apprenticeship*, p.433.

actual discoveries.'[1] This is partly because 'Most students seem to assume that it is the previous stage of making observations and taking notes which is that of discovery.'[2] If one used the metaphor of film, the editing stage, which is when one assembles the material into a new order, is widely known to be as important as the filming or 'collecting' stage. Yet most people do not realize this when undertaking literary work.

LOOSENING THE IMAGINATION

In an appendix to *The Sociological Imagination*, C.Wright Mills gives a number of descriptions of how he works. He describes how 'After making my crude outline I examined my entire file, not only those parts of it that obviously bore on my topic, but also those which seemed to have no relevance whatsoever. Imagination is often successfully invited by putting together hitherto isolated items, by finding unsuspected connexions. I made new units in the file for this particular range of problems, which, of course, led to new arrangements of other parts of the file.'[3]

What happens is that 'As you rearrange a filing system, you often find that you are, as it were, loosening your imagination. Apparently this occurs by means of your attempt to combine various ideas and notes on different topics. It is a sort of logic of combination, and "chance" sometimes plays a curiously large part in it. In a relaxed way, you try to engage your intellectual resources, as exemplified in the file, with the new themes.'[4] All

---

[1] WEBB, *Apprenticeship*, p.433
[2] WEBB, *Apprenticeship*, p.433
[3] WRIGHT-MILLS, C, *The Sociological Imagination*, Oxford: Oxford University Press (1959), p.221.
[4] WRIGHT-MILLS, *Sociological*, p.221.

sorts of things go into the original files, made possible by a very flexible storage system which '... encourages you to capture "fringe thoughts": various ideas which may be by-products of everyday life, snatches of conversation overheard on the street, or, for that matter dreams. Once noted, these may lead to more systematic thinking, as well as lend intellectual relevance to more directed experience.' These files contain 'ideas, personal notes, excerpts from books, bibliographical items, and outlines of projects.' This constitutes an ever-enriched resource. 'Then as you pursue your work you will notice that no one project ever dominates it, or sets the master categories in which it is arranged. In fact, the use of the file encourages expansion of the categories which you use in your thinking.'

Even the actual method of note-taking forces you to think about what you are doing. 'Merely to name an item of experience often invites you to explain it; the mere taking of a note from a book is often a prod to reflection.' The file is 'a continually growing store of facts and ideas, from the most vague to the most finished.' When one comes to write, it is really a development from these files: 'the idea and the plan came out of my files, for all projects with me begin and end with them, and books are simply organized release from the continuous work that goes into them.'[1]

The files lead to those unexpected associations and connections which we have seen are the essence of true discovery. In intellectual work, '...there is an unexpected quality about it, perhaps because its essence is the combination of ideas that no one expected were combinable – say a mess of ideas from

---
1 WRIGHT-MILLS, *Sociological*, pp.217-221.

German philosophy and British economics.'[1] The unexpectedness comes from the method of proceeding – the mind has broken apart and is now able to re-combine elements. 'On the most concrete level, the rearranging of the file, as I have already said, is one way to invite imagination. You simply dump out heretofore disconnected folders, mixing up their contents, and then re-sort them. You try to do it in a more or less relaxed way.'

The classifications created by the original materials can be broken. 'Many of the general notions you come upon, as you think about them, will be cast into types. A new classification is the usual beginning of fruitful developments.' So 'rather than rest content with existing classifications, in particular, common-sense ones, you will search for their common denominators and for differentiating factors within and between them. Good types require that the criteria of classification be explicit and systematic. To make them so you must develop the habit of cross-classification.'

Wright Mills realizes that linking things, connecting, or as he calls it 'cross-classification' is the key to discovery. 'For a working sociologist, cross-classification is what diagramming a sentence is for a diligent grammarian. In many ways, cross-classification is the very grammar of the sociological imagination.'[2]

What Wright Mills has described overlaps with the other descriptions. You extract, abstract, cross-relate, and re-integrate into new patterns. 'After you decide on some "release", you will try to use your entire file, your browsing in libraries, your conversation, your selections of people – all for this topic or theme. You are trying to build a little world containing all the

---

1 WRIGHT-MILLS, *Sociological*, p.233.
2 WRIGHT-MILLS, *Sociological*, pp.233-235.

key elements which enter into the work at hand, to put each in its place in a systematic way, continually to readjust this framework around developments in each part of it.'[1]

---

[1] WRIGHT-MILLS, *Sociological*, pp.245.

TWO

Conversation

THE MAJOR PART of what one learns about the world comes from talking to people. Conversation, or oral accounts, are central to our understanding and holding somewhat directed conversations and recording what one learns are the most important part of trying to gain a deeper understanding of our world.

In my Nepal fieldwork, for example, there have been a dozen or so key informants over the years, men, women and children who have guided our growing knowledge of their culture. Of these three or four took me really deep into their worlds and explained to me most of what I know. In Japan and China there have been similar experiences.

What is revealed through long conversations, joking, testing of guesses, shared confusion and sudden enlightenment, cannot be gained in any other way. The role of the deeply enmeshed local person who acts as a key informant is often alluded to in dedications to anthropology books. But seldom is it pointed out that most of the most valuable inside information we receive about a community tends to come from a handful, or just one or two, people.

Learning to interview people is an art, and like all arts it is learnt by practice and reflection on what does or does not work.

I had become interested in oral history and hearing people's stories early in my life through my grandmother's accounts of her life in Burma and India. This interest developed more explicitly during my time as a postgraduate at Oxford, where I began to learn the pleasure of talking to older people, my teachers in history and anthropology, about their lives.

So by the time I started my first fieldwork I had already learnt a few of the techniques of interviewing. These are fairly obviously stated, though more difficult to apply: attentiveness, curiosity without nosiness, appreciation of jokes, encouraging without pushing. The success will also depend on how much you already know. Talking about events and people to a totally ignorant outsider can be boring and frustrating. So the conversations improve as you develop local knowledge.

What began in the field as a number of interviews has expanded through my various fieldwork visits and continued in a considerable way at home in Cambridge. I have done film interviews of over 200 distinguished thinkers, almost all of which are available on the web, as described below.

* * *

Interviews are often divided into three types. There are structured interviews, with a set of questions formally asked and boxes filled in; semi-structured interviews, with a set of questions put informally and not in a particular order and people allowed freedom to go off onto other subjects; and informal interviews where people just talk about what they like. I find the semi-structured most useful. There are questions I want to cover, but I have found that if you sit with a piece of paper with a list of questions, and particularly if this means that you do not listen with attention to the answers and allow the interviewed person freedom to follow a train of thought away from the present subject, your subjects begins to feel used – milked of useful information, but not really engaged.

Of course timing is all. There are good times (and places) to talk, and there are right moments to break off the talking, or to postpone it. The more information you can give to the person you are talking to before you start the interview about why you are doing it and what constraints you mutually agree on the use of the information, the better.

It is very worthwhile to record an interview for later analysis. If you are going to do this, certainly since the advent of video cameras, you should, if possible, do this on film. Most communication is non-verbal, so to catch the smiles (or sneers!), the movement of the eyes, the pauses and shifts in expression adds hugely to the meaning of an interview. It also makes it both much easier – and more interesting – to transcribe if you want to do that later.

If you film, it is even more necessary to explain what you are doing and why. It is also important to make the presence of the camera as unobtrusive as possible. I dispense with lights, tripod, lapel mike. There may be some loss in technical excellence, but the gain in trust and intimacy far outweighs this.

There is also the question of length. I have tended to keep my interviews at between 30 and 120 minutes, enough to capture part of the life of a busy person in an afternoon. But I know that sometimes it is worth doing many hours of interview to catch the rich detail. In the interview I did with my principal informant in Nepal, Dilmaya Gurung, in order to avoid boredom or strain, I split up the interview into 20-30 minute sections, of which there were 12, so over six hours in all. In all cases I sat on the same level, on the ground, with the camera on my lap as if it was just a part of my body. This is what I have found best, just relaxing where the subject feels relaxed, talking to each other, while the camera soon merges into the background.

* * *

Here are some notes on how I have conducted the more than 200 interviews with academics and others. The interviews in the field with native informants are different, but overlap, so this guidance will help to explain the content of the featured interviews

On the surface, the interviews are almost unstructured and I avoid referring to a written questionnaire as this can distract from the spontaneity of the occasion. I encourage the interviewee to talk about whatever they would like. My role is similar to a psychiatrist, that is to say to let the subject narrate their life, in particular in relation to the obstacles and encouragements to creativity and discovery. We tend to cover the following.

- *When and where born*
- *Ancestry – going back as far as they like, including occupation and temperament and possible effects of grand-parents, parents and siblings*
- *First memories and hobbies as a child*
- *First and subsequent schools, with important teachers, hobbies, subjects which gripped them, sports and games, music, special books*

- *University and those who taught and studied with them and interests there*
- *First research, supervisors, mentors, influences*
- *Jobs and career and travels through life, work abroad*
- *Colleagues, friends and network of workers, partners and children*
- *Methods of working and thinking*
- *Major achievements and problem-solving during life, how they occurred, including especially important bursts of activity*
- *Administrative tasks*
- *Teaching and supervising of students*
- *Effects of their work environment (laboratories, departments, Colleges etc)*
- *Philosophy and religion*
- *Political views and activities*
- *Advice for a young person starting out in their field*
- *Specifically ask if there is anything which they would like to have talked about and I have omitted to ask about*

Yet if the subject does not want to follow this order, or to answer all of these, or to add further subjects, that is fine. What I want the viewer to see is the inside of a life, told in a conversational and personal way.

The interviews are an intimate probing of personal experience, usually by a complete stranger who is holding a potentially threatening video camera. The subjects know that this may be seen by almost anyone in the world - friends, students, competitors, and enemies, now and in the future. This could be intimidating, especially to older subjects and for those who share a widespread reserve and distaste for talking about themselves.

HOW TO STUDY THE WORLD

* * *

For those who would like to experience some of the film interviews I have made, here is a personal selection of twenty among those I have found particularly memorable, though many of the rest are fascinating too.

TWENTY SELECTED INTERVIEWS

I have put more than 200 film interviews up on the Cambridge University web-site.

http://upload.sms.cam.ac.uk/collection/1092396

Here are a selection of ten per cent of these – among those that I found particularly interesting to do. By going to the above web-site and typing in their name, you can watch the interview.

Allan Brigham studied history at University and then came to Cambridge, intending to stay for a few weeks. He has been in the city, which he has learnt to love, for many years and combines sweeping the roads, and taking visitors on tours of the city. He was awarded an honorary M.A. from the University for his services to Cambridge.

Sir John Eliot Gardiner is one of the world's greatest conductors. He studied at King's College Cambridge where his performance of Monteverdi's Vespers when he was still an undergraduate attracted international acclaim. He now conducts all over the world, often with his Monteverdi Choir.

Philippe Descola is a French anthropologist. He was supervised by Claude Lévi-Strauss for his doctorate in Paris and undertook more than two years of research among a remote tribe in the Amazon basin alongside his wife Anne Christine Taylor (of whom there is also an interview). His 'Spears of Twilight' is a brilliant account of this experience.

Clifford Geertz was one of the two or three best known anthropologists in the world. His work in Morocco and Indonesia and his contributions to cultural anthropology have had a huge influence on anthropology in the last half of the twentieth century.

Sir Brian Harrison was one of those whose methodology ('one fact one card') most influenced my early research. He has published widely, including editing the many volume *History of Oxford University* and was then the editor of the *Dictionary of National Biography*. He gives a particularly honest and thoughtful account of his childhood in London.

Hermann Hauser studied physics at Cambridge and was at the centre of the development of information technology, particularly the important development of micro-computers and networks in the 1970's. He then became the central figure in the development of the Cambridge Science Parks, and one of the leading 'Angel' investors in Britain.

Sir Gabriel Horn came from a poor, Jewish, tailor background in London and left school young. Through perseverance and hard work he ended up as one of the most important influence on the development of the Life Sciences in Cambridge in the second half of the twentieth century as Professor of Zoology, Master of Sidney Sussex College, founder of the Gurdon Centre.

Stephen Hugh-Jones was brought up in Jamaica and then sent to British public schools. He studied social anthropology under Edmund Leach and others at King's College, Cambridge and then spent many years as a Lecturer in Cambridge. He under-took outstanding fieldwork with his wife Christine in the Amazonian jungles and gives a particularly vivid account of this work.

Sir Tim Hunt was a year below me at the Dragon (Preparatory) School at Oxford and then went on to become one of the most distinguished biologists of the later twentieth century. His work on the ultimate building blocks of cells, the discovery of cyclin, gained him the Nobel Prize and he became an ambassador for Science. His retirement work was destroyed by a totally unwarranted campaign against him for a joke he made in Korea. The interview was made a few weeks after this event and he explains the background in detail.

Sir Aaron Klug worked himself up from a humble South African background to become one of the greatest scientists of the second half of the twentieth century. He won the Nobel Prize in Chemistry in 1982, and was not far off winning another three Nobel prizes. For example, he specified the methods which like behind CAT scans. He was for some years Director of the world-famous MRC laboratory at Cambridge.

Sir Geoffrey Lloyd studied classics at Cambridge and was for some years Senior Tutor at King's College, Cambridge and then

Master of Darwin College, Cambridge. He was internationally known as an expert on Greek philosophy and history, but later he decided to learn Chinese in order to compare ancient Chinese and Greek thought. He became the Chairman of the Board of the Needham Institute in Cambridge and an expert on two civilizations. His interview is almost totally without interruption – a perfectly formed oration.

David MacDougall is probably the leading theorist and innovator in ethnographic film in the world. His very long interview is a brilliant account of his early work developing new film techniques (for example the use of sub-texts for translating foreign languages) in his African work. He pioneered work on Aboriginal film in Australia and then made several important series of films about education in India.

David McLellan almost became a Jesuit monk, and describes his training. Instead he became perhaps the world's most important scholar of the work of Karl Marx, translating and editing a number of Marx's most important works, including the *Grundrisse*, and writing several important biographical pieces on Marx.

Sir Nicholas Phillips studied law at King's College, Cambridge, and is an Honorary Fellow of the College. He is one of the three most distinguished British judges of the twentieth century, being in turn Master of the Rolls, Senior Law Lord, Lord Chief Justice and then the first President of the newly formed British Supreme Court.

Lord Martin Rees is one of the most distinguished scientists of his generation. A Fellow of King's College he held many important positions, including Astronomer Royal, President of the Royal Society, Master of Trinity College, Cambridge. His books and television and radio appearances have had a widespread influence on many fields.

Sir Christopher Ricks was the English tutor at Worcester College, Oxford, when I was an undergraduate there and taught a number of my friends. He was known to be a formidable scholar of everything from the songs of Bob Dylan to the works of several great English Romantic poets, whose poems he edited. His sparkling wit is shown in a bravura performance.

Simon Schaffer has been a friend for over thirty years, involved in several joint projects and teaching in the Department of the History and Philosophy of Science which is next door to the Department of Social Anthropology. He is a world expert on seventeenth century science, especially the works of Boyle, Newton and their circles. He is also a charismatic television presenter and has been involved in several series on glass and the history of the world.

George Steiner is in many ways the nearest I have come to finding a Renaissance Man. Equally at home in Greek philosophy, Renaissance thought, modern continental literature, he has written numerous books exploring the delights and tragedies of our age. He gives a moving account of his life on the margins of academia in America, Britain and the Continent.

Sir Keith Thomas was my D.Phil. supervisor at Oxford and, as his first student, I received a wonderful education as he wrote, alongside my thesis on witchcraft, his seminal work, *Religion and the Decline of Magic*. He occupied many important positions in his life: President of Corpus Christi College, Oxford, Chairman of the Syndics of Oxford University Press, President of the British Academy.

Lord William Waldegrave was at Eton and Oxford, and comes from an ancient English noble family which at times owned the great house of the Walpole's at Strawberry Hill. He became a politician and served in the Conservative cabinet under Margaret Thatcher. Later he became Provost of Eton College. He is a distinguished book collector, academic and writer.

THREE

Experience: Participating and Observing

It is obvious that from the moment we are born, every human being becomes both a participant and an observer. We play our children's games, and watch ourselves playing them, we do a job, and watch ourselves doing the job. This is the universal and most powerful way of learning about the world.

Normally we learn to do this without any instruction. We may be encouraged to keep a diary, or to reflect on our lives in letters or our Facebook page. But we do not think too much about what we are doing when we engage in the productive tension between being part of events and thinking about them.

When anthropologists wanted to develop a method to understand very different societies to those in which they had been born, they decided to formalize this universal method. They would go to a far-away society and live there for some months or years, participating in the life of the community and, at the same time, observing it and recording it in their fieldnotes, diaries, photographs and films.

If we want to understand our highly diverse world, enjoy and appreciate different cultures to our own, or even just to survive the shocks when we enter new worlds within our own society (school, university, job, marriage), it is useful to think more explicitly about how we practice this participant-observation method.

I shall give an account of parts of how participation-observation works based on many periods of fieldwork around the world. For almost half a century I have tried to understand a changing mountain village in Nepal. For a quarter of a century I have tried to understand the world of the Japanese. For twenty years I have tried to understand the gigantic changes that are occurring in China. All of these attempts were based on longer or shorter periods of participant-observation.

Here is a very simple account of a powerful method to overcome a little of the distance which separates us from people who start as strangers, and then become friends. It is mainly based on my twenty visits to spend time with a group of people called the Gurungs in the Annapurna mountains in Nepal. But though at first this fieldwork site was remote and far away, the essence of the methods can apply anywhere.

PARTICIPANT-OBSERVATION FIELDWORK

Fieldwork resembles a 'rite of passage' or movement from one position to another, as in a wedding or funeral. There is a period when one leaves the familiar world, dis-embeds or dis-aggregates oneself. Then there is a period when one is in some kind of liminality or parallel world, out of normal space and time, yet maintaining a tension between participating and observing. Then there is the re-incorporation back into one's own world, yet a world in which you have changed, often very deeply.

One way of thinking about the experience of fieldwork is to think of it as like learning to swim. The aptness of the metaphors of learning the various useful strokes, the shock of immersion in a sometimes cold and alien element, the way in which all of one's body and senses are challenged, is obvious. But here I just want to mention another aspect of my own experience.

When I learnt to swim, the great break–through was when I realized that my body was naturally buoyant, when I learnt to relax and to float. I found I did not need to struggle, to paddle furiously, to fear drowning. I could stop striving, surrender myself to the water and just lie on the surface and enjoy the feeling of weightless security.

It is the same with participant-observation fieldwork. At first I feared the thought of failure, was wary of letting down my guard, jealously guarded my privacy and my principles, felt suspicious of overtures of friendship. I felt I could easily drown, and there was a panic that I would never collect enough material upon which to base my Ph.D.

I had survived boarding schools from the age of eight by striving and pushing as hard as I could. There was a tendency to feel that only through struggle would I do so in Nepal. But gradually, I recall, I relaxed and the fear of failure or cultural suffocation dropped away.

As with swimming, it is worth remembering that the people with whom you are living – or most of them – will support and advise you on how to swim. It is in their interest, and a matter of self-satisfaction, if you enjoy yourself, can communicate with them, and can perhaps share some of your own knowledge and contacts with them. So they will want you to succeed.

PARTICIPATING

The social scientist uses all of his or her self, head, heart, spirit and body. He or she becomes, in the excellent metaphor, a musical instrument upon which the culture plays. He feels, absorbs, shares as well as watches and questions. This is what makes anthropology and some branches of sociology special, and also particularly difficult. The archaeologist digs up artefacts which are separate from him, the historian visits repositories where he can sit and handle the books and papers, the sociologist devises surveys and questionnaires which can, if necessary, be done at a distance. In these and similar disciplines you **do** something. In anthropology you **are** something. You **do** history, you **are** an anthropologist. Anthropology is not just an academic discipline but a way of life, or as Claude Lévi-Strauss put it, along with music and mathematics, it is a *vocation*, a calling.

PARTICIPATING IN SOCIAL LIFE

In some ways, especially once I was adopted into a Nepalese (Gurung) family, participating in social life was the easiest and most enjoyable part of fieldwork. It was easy to play with children, to go to village dances and other social events, to participate in lineage picnics, to attend weddings and funerals, and to spend long evenings chatting with our family. The very nature of all these occasions was inclusive and participatory. The only problem, occasionally, was to be the observer while participating in something so all-involving and fun.

Clearly the most important thing on these social occasions is to show appreciation and enjoyment, to enter into the sense of fun. Usually this is easy, though occasionally the food or drink on offer had to be surreptitiously slipped away behind a convenient bush. The participating, of course, should be reciprocal. During our first fieldwork we bought large supplies of Horlicks, one of the few things that seemed to be available in the nearest town. Every evening we would invite any Gurungs who wanted to come into our little house to share it with us, chat, and, hopefully to sing. I would bring out my guitar and have sing-alongs with them – entertainment which was still remembered by our friends some forty years later.

The other thing about social participation was that one realized that all types of activity were basically social. Going out to work in the forests or fields was made tolerable, even enjoyable, by the fact that it was done in groups, members of whom would chat and joke and sometimes sing. Likewise ritual events such as a wedding or funeral, or a shamanic, Buddhist or Hindu ritual, were as much social as religious occasions.

Sometimes this was a surprise. I come from a Protestant country where the holy was also solemn and jollity was taboo. I had been taught not to chat or play in church services. To attend these clearly important rituals and to find everyone behaving as if was a secular, social, occasion – chatting, wandering around, breast-feeding babies, was surprising.

All of this reminded me through participating that I was in a society where the pretended separation of economy, politics, religion and society of 'modern' societies does not exist. Everything was mixed, religion and economics were social, and the social also had economic and religious significance.

I also discovered some of the rhythms of the year. We arrived in the winter when there was hardly any agricultural work to

All of this is set within a larger problem which is that you basically only know a little of what you don't know – where the gaps are – and do not know at all about many things which you have not even guessed are important – the 'unknown unknowns' in Donald Rumsfeld's formulation.

This can be put in another way. I found through my fieldwork that people would tend to tell me things which I had already guessed. They would not waste time and effort explaining to an uneducated and ignorant outsider what they clearly had no clue about. It would be a waste of breath and uninteresting. But if you surprise and intrigue them, starting to play the game at a better level, perhaps even contributing things they themselves did not know to the conversation, then a true intellectual exchange gets under way.

For example, if you asked blandly whether there were sometimes marriages between people who were proscribed from marrying each other, normally people would say no. But if you had worked out or guessed that such a marriage had taken place, you might, with a trusted person, cite this case and they might confirm it – and then give more instances.

It is part of the 'Catch 22' of all fieldwork. Until you know what you are looking for and are pretty sure it is there, you will not find it. It is very much a matter of hazarding guesses, often based on your wider comparative training and reading about what happens in other cultures, and then seeing if it is true in the one you are working in. As with a jigsaw puzzle, you have to have a mental picture of the shape and image of a missing piece before you will find it.

* * *

do and the social was at the forefront. I began to feel that the villagers were so relaxed and full of minor chatting and socializing that my expectation of hard work in a mountain village might be misplaced. But from about March or April the agricultural tasks picked up, reaching a peak in the transplanting of rice in the torrential rains of the monsoons, and then through weeding and harvesting until the festival of Dashain in October again issues in the leisured dry weather. I saw then that the grinding work, the festivals and dancing and social were mirrored parts of life.

PARTICIPATING IN PHYSICAL LIFE

Participating in the physical work of a community has several advantages. One is that you will show that by being prepared to do this you do not scorn but respect such work. Your very limited contribution is the result of lack of capacity, not some scorning of physical work.

Trying out each piece of work for a short period is also the one way to realize how extremely difficult even the simplest looking of tasks can be. They often require great skill and energy, but the people who have commanded these make it look easy, like all artists. It was not until I tried to plough, to hoe, to cut rice, or my wife tried to winnow grain or to weave with a backstrap loom, that we fully realized the incredible strength of even young people and frail-looking old people.

Until you try to carry over twenty kilograms of wood or animal manure a few yards up or down a mountain path you will not understand what village life is about, or fully see why most long for another, less stressful and demanding, life, with a chance of better pay and prospects.

Another reason for at least a limited participation in physical life is that in attempting to join in such tasks the roles are reversed. You are the student, they are the teachers. The observed become the observers and teachers, leaning over the shoulder metaphorically or actually, encouraging and criticizing. This is good for both of you.

Other parts of sharing in the physical life will happen just by living for an extended period in the host community. You will come to realize how exhausting the everyday grind of washing without washing machines, fetching water from an intermittent communal tap, climbing up to the village or further up to the forest, are. Of course, even sharing a little in the constant debilitating minor illnesses, the coughs, colds, sores, bites, leeches, sprains, which afflict people most of the time, is an education in itself.

PARTICIPATION IN EMOTIONAL LIFE

Perhaps the most demanding, yet rewarding, part of participation is emotional. It might be thought that from a very different background and with no preliminary links to people in the field, you will not feel deeply about those you are with. This is not our experience. We found very soon, and increasingly over our visits, that as the Bible enjoined us, we could 'Rejoice with them that do rejoice, and weep with them that weep.' The triumphs and tragedies in such a situation are more direct and affecting because there is little to screen other people. They are open and plain. A sick child, a lost animal, an exam success, the return of a friend from overseas, all are things everyone shares.

As John Donne noticed, the tendency towards individualism in Western culture cuts us off from each other. His reminder that 'no man is an island' is not needed in a communal society. You do not need to ask for whom the bell tolls. Within seconds or minutes of a death in a small community everyone knows and shares the pain.

It is perhaps here that the metaphor of the instrument upon which the culture plays is most apt. If you start to feel happiness, even joy, and sorrow, even anguish, when people you know in the field are affected by the slings and arrows of outrageous fortune, you will know that you have crossed over the huge abyss that seems to exist between individuals and cultures. You will then be able to begin to understand another world at a deeper, emotional, level.

Of course, as with all our social relations, you will be expected to show emotions which you do not feel – and the people do this themselves. For instance in the traditional wailing (keening) at funerals, some of it is heart-felt, some obligatory. You will soon learn what is expected.

You will also learn what is appropriate in terms of expressing emotion through physical contact. The rules about touching, kissing, cuddling are variable and a mis-placed gesture can lead to trouble. I was fortunate that the body-distances and the rules of cuddling and hugging among the people I worked with were reasonably familiar and easy to learn and apply.

PARTICIPATION IN MENTAL AND MORAL LIFE

Your thoughts are your own and you can keep them so. But there are many occasions when you will be asked for your views and opinions on aspects of local life. For instance, your view of the political authorities or local big men, of priests and of teachers. Or you may be asked to subscribe to ideas which in your own home culture you would think ridiculous, superstitious or discriminatory. You may be asked to believe someone is a witch, that someone has been cursed, that women or certain occupational groups are inferior, that certain things are taboo or have magical power.

Unless it offends your basic principles, it is best to practice the general technique of 'the willing suspension of disbelief.' For instance, with religious beliefs, including those in magic and witchcraft, if asked I would say that few people in England now believe in these things, but a few hundred years ago there was almost universal belief.

If asked about women or so-called 'Untouchables' you can usually stick to your principles, especially within your own private living space. Villagers knew that any Dalits (untouchables) could come into our house and that if we visited their houses we would accept food and drink from them.

On the other hand, there is no point in being aggressively belligerent. It is unlikely that your preaching or extreme action will change a general view. In some ways anthropology is based on the reversal of Karl Marx's famous dictum that 'Our task is not to understand society, but to change it.' Anthropologists tend to be free of the heavy burden of international aid works or missionaries. They do no have to convert people, win their hearts, show them the error of their ways or improve them. They are there to extend mutual understanding, and that means getting inside the logic of unfamiliar and often initially abhorrent beliefs. Usually when you understand the premises and the outcomes, you will be more tolerant, even if, in the end, you still personally reject both the premises and the consequences.

PARTICIPATION IN RITUAL LIFE

Beliefs and ideas are manifested in ritual and other forms of religious action. Many smaller communities around the world have a rich ritual life which can provide quite a shock to someone who comes from the West, especially if it is from the relatively ritually diminished part of Protestant northern Europe or America. Suddenly you find yourself invited to events filled with gestures and actions which you do not understand at all, and encouraged to participate in them – to be sprinkled with animal blood or encouraged to drink cow's urine, or to lay wreaths on obviously phallic objects.

I still remember that when this first happened to me in the field I felt confused about what I should do. My Protestant upbringing told me it was all mumbo-jumbo. The same upbringing made me feel that it would be hypocrisy to go through the rituals as if I believed them, and, at worst, it would be a form of idolatry, a betraying of my Christian roots.

Quite soon, however, I relaxed. External actions and inner beliefs are different. You can offer small gifts to a Brahmin without being a Hindu. You can offer a small chicken to a village godling without losing your religious purity. This relativistic view was made much more acceptable by watching my friends in this pluralistic religious universe. One moment they might be doing a puja, apparently devout Hindus, the next they might be attending a lamaistic funeral, apparently devout Buddhists, and then in the evening they might invite in the pre-Buddhist shaman to do an anti-witchcraft ritual. They did not see this as inconsistent.

What I discovered was that my over-simplified western cosmology, which not only demarcated religion and made it 'holy' and 'sacred,' but also monotheistic and a strict combination of ethics, doctrine, beliefs about the after life and ritual behaviour into one bundle, was not applicable in much of the world.

I found I was in the majority world, away from the Judeo-Christian-Islamic, often intolerant, exclusive and proselytizing monotheisms. In the great world of Asia there is no real approximation to what we mean by 'Religion,' while at the same time 'religion' is everywhere.

This explained not only the multiple and apparently non-conflicting, pluralistic, religions in the village, but also the fact that supposedly religious occasions were not set apart, discrete, like church services would be in the West. I remember tentatively asking if I could photograph, even film, and take notes during a *puja*. People said, of course. Rituals are also, as we have seen, economic and social events. They are much more like what I have read about Catholicism in some rural areas of the Mediterranean or Latin America.

As I relaxed and felt no inhibition in filming even solemn occasions such as burning a body or shamanic possession, I realized how wonderful this opportunity was. Rituals are orchestrated for people to join in – it is a form of participation which expresses community solidarity. Observing and recording rituals was a chance, for a moment, to see hitherto hidden tensions and relations in a society made manifest. Because so much is happening so fast and in so many places, filming rituals and then watching the film again is not only one of the few ways both to convey an important part of village life to outsiders, but also to allow you to re-examine in slow motion what is happening.

Another point again derives from my Protestant background. I was taught that I should understand the meaning of what I was participating in. As I learnt my Christianity, the point and underlying purpose of the ceremonies was explained to me. They were all in English and I could follow them and thought I could understand the symbolism.

When attending rituals in Nepal it all seemed mysterious and confused. Why was this done, what was the meaning of that symbol? It seemed somehow to be cheating, or at the best I was left outside the event, if I could not begin to understand it.

Of course one of the joys of fieldwork is that what on the first occasion seems totally meaningless confusion can begin to be understood. When you see it again, you begin to realize that the actions are not random, the relationships can be understood.

But it is worth remembering that you may not be the only one who does not understand what is going on. I have often asked my Gurung friends how much they understand of what is going on in a complex ritual and very often they answer with the local equivalent of 'I haven't a clue.' They do not understand the old language of the shamans. They do not know enough about the theoretical side of Buddhism or Hinduism to understand much of what is happening.

* * *

A final point is that the whole essence of ritual was difficult for me to grasp from the viewpoint of a western Protestant. The essence of ritual is the idea that through the manipulation of matter – through sounds, smells, gestures, sacrifices and so on – a human can somehow change or affect an invisible spiritual world. You can ward off a witch with a spell or sacrificed chicken, you can improve the harvests by worshipping a local goddess.

Now this whole system, both the part which envisages a parallel world of spiritual forces just on the edge of our consciousness, a sort of wireless wavelength which we cannot see or control without the 'ritual radio,' and the part which says that we can force or cajole these forces into altering their course by doing things, runs against the last several hundred years of Protestant culture.

For me, coming from a world which had strictly separated this world of matter from that of God and the spirits, which had rejected miraculous intervention, masses, candles and saints and the conversion of wine into blood, it all seemed mumbo-jumbo.

It took a real effort to re-enter an enchanted world where the spiritual forces are just behind the surface. I had once inhabited such a world as a child, a world where fairies and Father Christmas and talking animals were my companions. But from about the age of twelve onwards this had withered. Now in my fieldwork I had to re-enter a magical world. By so doing, entering the door once through a number of fieldwork visits to Nepal, I suddenly found it possible to do the same in a more dramatic and unexpected way in my work on Japan, where the spiritual forces or *kami* were lurking hidden behind the bullet trains, pachinko parlours and department stores.

All of this reinforces earlier remarks about how much we have to change in ourselves if our fieldwork is going to be helpful in seeing the world anew. It does not mean that we have to lose our convictions and beliefs. I am still an agnostic Protestant, still an academic individualist, still a believer in the basic unity and equality of human beings. But I have also travelled in alternative lands, entered magic casements. Doing so has, in some strange way, made my own world a little more unexpected, surprising and, dare I say it, magical too.

OBSERVING

The other side of participant-observation is observing. This encompasses both the observation through one's eyes and ears and other senses, and also watching one's own interactions and conversations with people. It is a matter of standing above the participation and thinking about what is going on.

I have noted some of the difficulties in observing religion and of observing some particular segments of the community – women, children, the poor or lower caste. There are also problems in observing certain activities. Among the Gurungs, for example, eating in the house was a rather private matter and formal attempts to observe it, for example by filming or asking too many questions or, as in our first fieldwork, getting two young Gurung friends to note down what was eaten every day, can cause offence. Likewise, though much of the micro-politics of the village – informal settlements of arguments, school governor's meetings, meetings of the village Panchayat (council) when there was one - are public and one can observe them, other parts, family quarrels for example, may be sensitive.

An obvious fact is that while people may be happy for you

to be present and observe with your eyes, if you start explicitly to record the events with a view to remembering them, either by writing notes or by using a recorder or camera, people may feel uncomfortable or angry. If you are in doubt about this, you should always ask what is appropriate. If you also make your recording methods as unobtrusive as possible, though not invisible, using a very small notebook with infrequent jottings, a small recorder or camera, that all helps. Of course you should explain why you are observing and obtain the due informed consent, which is at the heart of ethical fieldwork.

The main philosophical difficulty with observation concerns the inter-connected questions of what to observe and what the meaning is of what you observe. As described with complex rituals, at first much of what goes on will be something of a blur. You cannot see how it works, what it means, what is essential and what is surface decoration. You have to direct your attention to a part, but which part?

If you know in advance that you will be observing an important and complex occasion and already have a trusted and helpful friend, it may help to obtain some 'notes' in advance, as one often does when going to an opera or musical performance. In other words, to go through with them the likely events and establish a rough shape of what will happen and especially what you should look out for. Then, when it is over and you come to write it up, if you have the time and energy, go through what happened and ask them about particular puzzles.

* * *

Obviously what you concentrate on observing and recording will depend on your own interest and project. Yet it is a general fact that anthropologists tend to observe and record much more than at first seems strictly necessary. This is partly because they know that in many societies you cannot divide off a particular area, such as the economy or religion, and ignore the rest, and partly because at least in much of the fieldwork, you do not know what is irrelevant, so it seems best to record on a broad front.

Another reason is that you may feel an obligation to observe and record a changing world because you know that if you do not do so, it is gone for ever. You cannot enter the same river of time twice. This came out in my experience of the contrast with history. You can note part of a book, or extracts from a document in an archive and be selective. If, later, you realize you have missed something, or your questions have changed, you can go back again if necessary.

You cannot do this in fieldwork. Unlike history or archaeology or most of the sciences, you create your own data, and if it is not created it does not exist independently of you. The moment passes, the society changes. Since it is a feature of all academic research that your questions are constantly changing as you learn more, you cannot afford to ignore materials merely because they are not currently part of your central question. You never know when some small, apparently trifling and irrelevant remark or observation, may suddenly be a key to further understanding.

RECORDING

The fieldwork is in many ways like trawler fishing. You go out with your nets of understanding and questions and try to gather what you can. The 'catch' will be frozen or salted and taken home to be dissected, cleaned and cooked in the 'writing-up' period, often as long or longer than the fieldwork.

Since the methods of anthropological recording overlap quite considerably with community style sociology, there is a fairly large literature which describes how it is best undertaken. In anthropology, the key form of documentation is descriptive – the fieldwork diary, notes and letters to friends. Yet the census, genealogies and maps, the economic, social and religious structured and semi-structured surveys, the interviewing and oral history, the work with two or three key informants, sound recordings, photography and filming, each of these is an art and requires care and attention to make it effective. If you come back with shoddy and poorly structured materials, it is likely to lead to shoddy and poorly structured writing.

Re-imagining the World

FOUR

Imagining

ONE OF THE most difficult yet important areas to consider is the process of turning the memories from our experiences and the notes from our recording of what we have seen, heard and read, into a new synthesis. Most of this happens at a level which we cannot easily observe. All I can do here is to describe a little of what I think happens, with particular reference to my experience of fieldwork in other societies, and to lay out before the reader a little of the magical moment when we turn our experience into a communication with others, through writing or other forms of art.

THE ORDERING OF CONFUSION

In some ways, the most difficult 'fieldwork,' certainly in anthropology and the social sciences, and to a considerable extent also for the historian, occurs in one's study when one 'returns' from collecting the primary materials, as Evans-Pritchard explains.

> *'I have had much, too much, field-experience, and I have long ago discovered that the decisive battle is not fought in the field but in the study afterwards. Any one who is not a complete idiot can do fieldwork, and if the people he is*

working among have not been studied before he cannot help making an original contribution to knowledge. But will it be to theoretical, or just to factual, knowledge? Anyone can produce a new fact; the thing is to produce a new idea." [1]

What Evans-Pritchard is alluding to is the creative re-ordering and reconstruction of the experience, the *Remembered Village*, which is caught in the title of Srinivas' book.[2] Manuals on method and autobiographies by social scientists seldom pay much, if any, attention to this stage, yet it is often as long and, in some ways, intense and arduous as the actual physical fieldwork.

The reason it is ignored, I suppose, is because it all occurs in the mind and there is not much dramatic external activity. From the outside, all that can be seen is someone at a desk, or in an easy chair, sorting out bits of paper, or scribbling, or typing. They are staring vacantly, or going for walks, or chatting to others. All of the complex activity, the reliving of the interviews, the re-experiencing and ordering of the many sensations, happens in the brain and imagination. So it is not only impossible to observe, but also difficult to write about.

What is there to say? Perhaps I can start on a personal note with my own experience. I spent about eighteen months in a small Yorkshire house surrounded by my little library and my fieldnotes and photos while day after day I would try either to analyse the material in a preliminary way, preparing it for writing, or in writing draft after draft of the thesis.

---

[1] EVANS-PRITCHARD, E. E, 'Some Reminiscences and Reflections on Fieldwork', *Journal of the Anthropological Society of Oxford* (1973), 4: p.3
[2] SRINIVAS, M.N, *The Remembered Village*, Berkeley: California University Press. 1976

ASSEMBLING THE JIGSAW

The data for academic work, whether that of the historian or anthropologist, comes to us in bundles, a whole interview, text, film, census or diary entry – but when constructing the thesis or book, different parts of the bundle need to go in different parts of the final work.

The material also comes in a higgledy piggledy fashion, different sources bearing on the same subject, bits of relevant material popping up at different parts of the fieldwork. Organizing it properly is essential.

And it is also the case that much of what we gather is only very partially understood at the time of recording and observing. This is partly because we know very little at the start, as well as having linguistic problems; but also because, in an interwoven social community, it is only when the context is understood and the bits linked together, that it will make any sense.

In a way, when I returned from fieldwork in the Himalayas I found myself with a huge jigsaw puzzle, one with hundreds of thousands of pieces jumbled up in my folders and files. There were many thousands of sense impressions, snippets of memory, bits of paper. The information was randomly stowed away in my mind, field notes and visual recordings. Nor did I have more than a faint suspicion of what the final picture represented by the parts might look like. I started out more or less blind but with a few hunches.

The first thing, as with a jigsaw, was to start to arrange the pieces. With a jigsaw you first get the edges in one place, then group certain striking colours or obviously identifiable things into other piles. There is a good deal of work to be done on the frame and the separations into likely sub-parts before you begin.

It is the same when you arrive back from the field. You spend some months 'sorting out the field notes.' This often consists of 'indexing' them in some way. For example, you might make a name index so that you can find everything about a person, or in putting colour stickers or other marks on long texts so that you can easily see when there is material about certain sub-themes, rituals, economics, social relations.

There are stories told of how Malinowski's students were encouraged to take out different coloured pencils to the field so that as the 'facts' arrived they could be written down or underlined in different colours. I heard this from Audrey Richards, and came across an example of this in action in Hortense Powdermaker's vivid account of her fieldwork.[1] This seems to me part of the process, and shows that the indexing can and perhaps should start in the field.

Yet it is also based on a rather strange idea, namely that you will know at that point – or ever – what is strictly economic, social or religious. The very nature of a holistic community is that most things, as Malinowski well knew, are *simultaneously* economic, social, religious and political. This was famously described in the concept of 'The Gift,' by Marcel Mauss,[2] and applies to all words, actions and objects we observe.

---

[1] POWDERMAKER, HORTENSE, *Stranger and Friend, The Way of an Anthropologist.* New York: Norton & Company, (1966) p.80.
[2] MAUSS, MARCEL, *The Gift, forms and functions of exchange in archaic societies* (London: Routledge and Kegan Paul, 1954)

FILING AND INDEXING

When in 1970 I was writing up my first fieldwork among the Gurungs in central Nepal there was no way I could use a computer for text searching. All the materials were on paper, in photographs, or in my mind, and it was tedious to search for things or to group them together for a piece of writing. It was all a matter of shuffling cards, indexing, starting to create mental and actual maps and diagrams.

The ultimate aim of all this work was that when I started to write the thesis, I would not have to search through heaps of notes to find the half-remembered or half-forgotten information.

The methods I adopted were aided by my previous experience and a love of filing systems. They worked for me, even if there was a huge effort. I managed, on the whole, to avoid a danger which has affected many of my own Ph.D. students returning from the field, namely the turning of weeks into months and months into years as they sort out their material and put off the writing.

This is a serious writing block caused by many factors. There is a protection from the nagging of supervisor or family for a while because you can say you are ordering the material, but simultaneously there is the circular anxiety as you begin to realize the size of the task ahead of you. The more you organize, the larger and more complex it seems to become.

TURNING HUMAN LIVES INTO PAPER

Where should you start? How do you know where you are going? What is the real question and set of hypotheses which should decide which bits of data are relevant and which should be put on one side?

Added to this, and seldom discussed, is the growing realization that what you are forced to do, and this applies even more to a thesis than to subsequent books, is to turn the glittering river of a vivid year or more's experience into a dry, stony, river-bed which one or two people only – your examiners and possibly the reader of an abstruse article or two – will walk down one day.

You are engaged in shredding and desiccating, reducing humans and life to jargon and statistics or dry texts, imposing artificial separations required by academic discourse on the lived reality. The seamless gown, the very essence of a non-western world you have experienced, has to be torn apart arbitrarily. You have to abstract and generalize. It is indeed a painful process and quite often students give up in despair or limp on, feeling inadequate and frustrated, year after year. Again the de-humanizing effect of writing is well described by Evans-Pritchard.

> *'It may be here that I should make a protest about anthropologists' books about peoples. A certain degree of abstraction is of course required, otherwise we would get nowhere, but is it really necessary to just make a book out of human beings? I find the usual account of field-research so boring as often to be unreadable – kinship systems, political systems, ritual systems, every sort of system, structure and function, but little flesh and blood. One seldom gets the impression that the anthropologist felt at one time with the people about whom he writes'* [1]

The months of starting to write up were difficult. Above all I

---

[1] EVANS-PRITCHARD, 'Some Reminiscences', p.12.

found it difficult to be constantly trying to re-imagine myself back into the field as I wrote. In order to go through this second fieldwork, you have to reverse the emphasis. The fieldwork puts participation first, and then there is the observation and a little analysis. In the writing phase, the participation is gone, except in your imagination. You are almost purely observing. And what are you observing? You are looking through a telescope at a receding landscape, struggling to keep the images alive: it is a process captured in a few lines at the end of Keats' 'Ode to a Nightingale' where after *'Opening magic casements on fairy lands forlorn,'* the poet is summoned back into this world by the word *'Forlorn'* and asks,

'Was it a vision, or a waking dream?
Fled is that music: – Do I wake or sleep?'

Yet as you start to move through the labyrinth of your mind, you begin suddenly to see where a piece of the jigsaw might fit; begin to see new patterns and connections of which you had not been aware in the field. As I wrote, I began to feel the pleasure of turning disorder into order, of turning confusion into understanding things which had at the time made no sense. So the writing started to gather momentum and I seemed to be making discoveries, finding out new things which no-one else had previously noticed. The work turned from a mechanical sorting and establishing of a background, to something more creative and even, occasionally, inspiring. I started to wake up wanting to write and re-write.

LIVING IN PARALLEL UNIVERSES

Part of the strain of the return is thus clearly that I was living a schizophrenic life. I had to re-adapt to what often felt like trivial practical matters, how to pay for my time and the family groceries, how to interact with other people who knew nothing of what I had gone through.

There was also a growing realization that, even if I obtained my Ph.D., that assured nothing. I needed to start to make a name for myself, give papers, publish, write reviews, network with useful contacts. All this has to be done to make oneself attractive on the job market, but all of it feels like a distraction, an interruption from the real work.

The schizophrenia was because alongside the practical existence of living in the West, you had to keep the fieldwork experience nourished and alive, otherwise the writing-up would fail. It was an effort to do so, but it was in many ways not unlike the effort of any artist – musician, painter, poet, novelist, who lives in a double world.

One difference from more flexible and creative artists who construct their own worlds, though related to life, was that you were not meant to invent anything. Proust or others could reconstruct their memories, or invent new ones. We ethnographers were meant to be objective, 'scientific.' If we did not have the information to back up our statements, we could not make it up. It was a peculiar position, made all the more peculiar for me in anthropology by comparing it to my first doctorate.

When I was writing up my Oxford history D.Phil. in a shed in the Lake District I tried to enter through my imagination the world of seventeenth century witchcraft. Yet I did not feel the same tension and strain. In the history case my mind and imagination lived in two worlds. This was true with anthropology too, but there was the added dimension that in anthropology my heart and emotions were also divided. Every time I planned and wrote about the intense experiences in my Himalayan village, I was there emotionally, as well as intellectually. I went through some of the feelings and thrill of participation.

This was not the case with writing on topics in the early modern period. I never learnt to love or hate (in a personal way) any of my seventeenth century authors. I did not even have a strong image of them. I could not hear their voices or watch their children playing. I never smelt, tasted or struggled physically in their world as I had done in the Himalayas.

When I wrote my second Ph.D., this time in a small house in the Yorkshire Dales, the 'writing-up' was tough in a different way to history, and not helped by the absence of any advice or explanation by any of my teachers or senior colleagues. We did not discuss the writing up *process* so I struggled alone – but watching my many Ph.D. students going through the same thing, I feel it may be helpful to start to try to analyse some of the difficulties and to explain to them how it may be made a little easier.

FIVE

Writing

THERE ARE A few very obvious but basic things about sustained creative work habits which I learnt early on; and though I sometimes break the rules, they generally guide me. One is to do with peace and a private space. It is important to have a place or places which are associated with writing; in my case this involved being in bed for the diary, at the desk for typing up, in an easy chair for original writing. This is why I wrote my first D.Phil. in a garden shed in the Lake District and my fieldwork Gurung Ph.D. in a small attic room at the top of a small house in a then quite remote Yorkshire village. And it is important that these places are, if possible, separated off from distractions and interruptions – especially difficult nowadays with mobile phones and Internet.

Then there is the question of how we write. This is very personal. My earlier writing was mainly on a typewriter. The second draft had to be completely re-typed as did every subsequent draft. So I improved a great deal from draft to draft. This filtering has disappeared with word processors, which produce a more or less perfect-looking (and spell-checked) version straight away. This makes it difficult to improve very much from version to version; tinkering seems both unnecessary and a big effort.

Although it slows things down – perhaps its great advantage

– I now only go straight to the 'typing into a computer' when I am writing short pieces, reviews or articles, where I already have a strong idea of what I want to say before I sit down to write. More extended pieces I write by hand with a pen. This forces me to re-type the text and at that stage it can be expanded or shrunk, the expression improved, new ideas inserted. It is a partial re-writing. It also means that it is easier to insert bits of writing done on a journey or elsewhere, when thoughts come but the laptop computer is not at hand.

There are other advantages. Even with the best of computers there is a danger of losing files. A hand-written version is the securest back-up. Also, perhaps because of my background, although I am a touch typist and can work fast without noticing the computer very much, it is always there. Simultaneously one is writing and being presented with what one has written. One mis-types more often than one mis-writes, so there are constant interruptions to go back and get it looking good, correct typos and grammar. This is taking away some of the energy that should be going into creativity. There is usually a hardly audible electronic buzz which is distracting.

I have found from experience that before starting to write it is helpful to have another sheet of paper, or, even better, some small slips, beside me. On these I jot down these intrusive thoughts. Once written down, the thought can be put on one side and dealt with later.

A serious obstacle is the feeling that we cannot proceed unless we do something else first. Often this is clearly just an excuse, which comes from the fact that writing and thinking are hard work. We want to be tempted, and if the temptation is an apparently reasonable one, such as the feeling that we cannot possibly write another word until we have read something in the library, or checked on the Internet, or talked to someone, it is very difficult to resist. Even the desire to go off and consult our own notes can lead to several hours' interruption, and the thread can be lost.

So I advise myself and my students to separate off the process of creative writing from the task of searching for data. If in my writing I come to a place where evidence or further consultation is needed, I make a guess and a note to myself to check something later. It is important to keep on with the sketch, even if certain things are missing, so 'to check' or 'to read X and Y' are put in and I work around the obstacle, to come back later to it. C.S.Lewis said research is like eating a fish; the bony parts could be taken out and put on the edge of the plate, to be dealt with carefully after the main part had been eaten.

AVOIDING BLOCKED PATHS

Another thing I have found helpful is to work on several different pieces of creative work at once. I did this with my history D.Phil and have continued to do so. The mind is multi-tasking and works better, I have found, on parallel problems. So usually I am working on a number of intellectual tasks simultaneously; for example, several different chapters of a book, several different books, and several different stages in the writing and re-typing of a work I am engaged on.

This has several advantages. If I am working on not just one but several chapters of a book or thesis, if I become stuck on one, I can leave it and move to another which may be more promising. We always get stuck and it often only requires leaving something for a while to solve the problem. The mind finds a way round without being forced. If we are only going down one path, we will be blocked. If we go down several simultaneously, we will progress all the time. We often find that we come back from behind the problem, and it has been outflanked and solved by working on something else.

Another advantage of working on several things at once is that different tasks require different types of concentration. To be writing the first draft of something, the first cutting through the undergrowth, is the most tiring and difficult. All is fresh and overgrown and confused.

Anthony Trollope rightly warned that we should not ever write at this high intensity for more than three hours a day. If we were to write for just these three hours, even a slow writer will produce about two thousand words a day, and hence in five days ten thousand words. In theory, it should be possible to write an eighty-thousand word book or thesis in two months, leaving the week-ends free! I have occasionally done something like this, but it seldom seems to works quite like this.

In fact, as well as working on the first draft of several different bits, there are other tasks. There is the typing in of the second version, or the reading through of a draft to make amendments, or the further reading and research. All these tasks need to be shuffled and varied over the days and weeks.

I have learned that it is best to work in parallel, rather than in blocks. It looks logical to write for a month, then spend a month reading or indexing, and then back to writing. Yet this does not work so well for me. I find I can only write at full concentration for about two or three hours on a first draft. Since my best time for writing is about 8-11 am, the creaming off of the best intellectual energy each day is far better than spending a week trying to write for six hours a day so that the next week I can read for six hours a day. So I ration my writing, but try to make sure that I stick at it.

Once we have allocated our best mental time to writing (for others it is late at night or early in the morning) that still leaves another four or five hours when the mind is active. If I am not teaching, administering, or, increasingly, answering emails, then I try to do a diversity of things, some reading (again I find two or three hours a day is enough), some note taking or indexing, some teaching or talking to people.

ENJOYING THE WRITING

Great artists, painters, poets, musicians, create almost subconsciously or by instinct. As academic writers, we can easily become over-cerebral, over-rational, over-conscious as we learn the craft. This is a necessary stage, but gradually it should become more instinctive. We hesitate, we try to get everything straight in our minds, everything sorted out first, and then to write. This often turns into a form of 'writer's block.'

I had this disease quite badly for a number of years. Being of only average ability, I knew that my undergraduate essays and later the drafts of my doctorate could only have a chance of competing with those of my brighter colleagues if I tried really hard and used superior organization. So I would not start to write until I had assembled a very detailed plan, down to the paragraph level. Each paragraph was mapped out and suitable quotes and arguments written out. Then the whole was embarked on. There was little spontaneity in most of the writing, though it did help to give a plausible semblance of intelligence.

It is obvious that some ideas, plans, plots are necessary before writing. But certainly as we gain confidence and experience, there is a wonderful liberation, and hopefully improvement, in our writing. We put down more of what we ourselves think, and then modify and delete it in the light of further thought and evidence.

In order to do this we have to have both confidence and enthusiasm in what we are doing. If we over-work or write, or have other deep worries, that undermines energy and enthusiasm and the writing suffers, and this then feeds back into the anxiety.

* * *

Although it seems logical to write in the order of the projected work, starting with a preface, chapter one, chapter two and proceeding on, in fact it is better to start somewhere in the middle, where the hub or centre of interest will be.

If I am lighting a fire, I do not start with the bigger, thicker, possibly wetter and more difficult branches, but with whatever will catch light most easily. Once this is alight, I can add thicker bits to the flame.

So start with whatever really excites you, the bit you think is the most entrancing, intriguing, amazing and mysterious. Then work out from that as the mind dictates. Do not start from the boring edges of a painting, but from the striking centre and then work out. This will help prevent artist's block and as you write or create you will gain confidence and excitement, which should grow until, without really noticing it, most of the work is roughed out. You can then tackle the most difficult and important pieces, the introduction and the conclusion, both of which should be written at the end.

Once the mind is aflame, let the flames leap as they wish. Do not try to limit or direct them too much. In other words, in Kipling's words, 'never write short.' Even if the writing goes in unpredictable directions and seems to be taking you away from your main aim, let it flow. It can always be pruned, cut, used elsewhere. But creative, excited, 'following the scent' writing, is a precious thing. When the mind is in full chase it should be encouraged, not reined in. Writing is a 'second fieldwork' or discovery, pursues clues and ideas as you write, in an amazing but subterranean way. Have trust in the mind and it may well come up in a strange, new, beautiful and fresh valley.

In other words, do not worry in the first draft about word lengths, chapter lengths, days elapsing before you get onto what you think is the real subject. The periods of writing enthusiasm never last for ever and often suddenly stop. When they do so, like a light switch being turned off as Kipling puts it, there is no point in forcing the mind on. Stop there and start or continue with something else.

KEEPING THE FLOW

If I am using a bonfire to burn a lot of rubbish over several days, I do not let the fire go out completely overnight. At the end of a day I leave a few half-burnt logs smouldering. It is much easier to start a new fire by raking over these live ashes and adding more wood rather than from scratch. The same is true of creative work. I learnt long ago from W.G.Hoskins, the local historian, that if I was going to leave some writing, for a night, and more especially for a few days, I should resist the temptation to tidily finish off a chapter or section. Starting at a blank page titled 'Chapter 3' at nine o'clock on a Monday morning after a break freezes the mind and makes it very difficult to get going.

It is much better to do most of the work, but leave a little bit to be done, with some brief notes as to where you think you will next go. Then, with the still warm argument raked over by re-reading the last few paragraphs you wrote, plus the indications of what to write next in your notes, you can continue for a few hours. The mind is now heated up and the transition to a new chapter or section feels much easier.

* * *

When you are in fully creative mood, ideas may come thick and fast. Hopefully they will form at 'the tip of your pen' (W.B. Yeats), but you will find that they also come at unexpected times through the day and night. Again they are often very transitory. Though you think you will remember them, they often flit off unless recorded. Especially in that precious moment between sleeping and waking in the morning when many ideas seem suddenly to crowd into the mind.

When I am in a creative mood, I try to carry a pen and small notebook, or even just some scraps of paper, with me. My mother tells me that from my early teens I used to carry a small tin filled with cards in it around with me. I called it pretentiously my 'Great Thoughts' box, which was later replaced by other similar systems. I now have little piles of paper around me to write on, as well as notebooks of various sizes.

I have noted that productive people of the generation above me, including a number of eminent scientists, seize envelopes, committee agendas or whatever is at hand and start to scribble on them. Thoughts are obviously darting into their minds. This is one of the joys of creativity. It is like fishing. You set the bait, relax, sit back, and, when you least expect it, there is a strong tug and you reel in to see what has been hooked.

FROM 'WRITING UP' TO 'IMAGINED COMMUNITIES'

When anthropologists come back from their fieldwork they often refer to the period when they work through their notes and memories and write the thesis or book as 'Writing Up.' Departments arrange 'Writing Up' seminars for those coming back from 'the field,' where they read rough chapters of their Ph.D. to each other and more senior scholars. This 'writing up' may go on for years.

The analogy here is perhaps with an earlier form of archaeology or history, or even the 'writing up' of results after an experiment in physics or chemistry. It is worth concluding by pointing out that such a metaphor, implying a fairly mechanical process of writing a formal account of the 'discoveries' already made, as a kind of report on gathered 'facts,' is deeply misleading.

The period in the field is an active one where there is much confusion, semi-understanding, unfinished business in the mind. Leaving the field one does not have a box of found artefacts, or ready-made pages of 'facts' copied down in a library or archive, or a set of 'results' from the laboratory. Instead one mainly has memories of sensations and experiences, only very partially embedded or made external on paper, film, tape or computer disc. Over ninety percent of what one has learnt is not yet synthesized or organized in the mind.

So the process when you return, the collating, listing, connecting, comparing with other personal experiences and other academic works, is just as important, if not more so, than the gathering phase. If we compare it to any form of art – writing a novel, writing a poem, painting, sculpture – we can immediately see that it is the period of reflection, and the struggle to understand and then to communicate our understanding to others, that is the central process. Without the lived experience, nothing worthwhile could be written. Yet without the self-examination and articulation afterwards, nothing of value will emerge.

These observations apply to all the social sciences, but from my experience in historical research, I think it is especially the case with anthropology. Really good anthropology is more difficult than any other social science, being so subjective and forcing you to move so from your known world. You have to make a double journey, out of your own world and cosmology into that of another set of people. You have to become enough like them to enter their way of being, without losing your own deeper foundations. Living in such a suspended, liminal, state for months, you change greatly and look at your own world afresh.

Then you return, trying to bring some of that newly found world with you, and try to recreate it both in your own mind and imagination and for your audience. It is the same task that faced Shakespeare and Milton, Dickens and Tolstoy, Rembrandt and Goya in other forms. When the fieldwork and re-imagining works, it is, like all creative work, one of the deepest and richest experiences of life. Yet it is not easy, and not made easier if you enter the process thinking that all that is involved is the 'writing up' of what you already know.

The true test of success is to compare the time when you 'returned' from the fieldwork, and the period when the text is completed. If the finished project is not almost entirely different from what you knew when you started to write, if it is not far richer than anything you could have written in the first few weeks, it is likely that what you will have achieved is perhaps something useful – the collection of some new bits and pieces. Yet it is unlikely that the finished project will expand our deeper knowledge of human beings and their diversity and similarities, the true goal of anthropology.

Explaining the World

What we find in our encounters with the world, and how we construct it into a work that communicates the experience to others, depends on what questions we are asking. This in turn depends on the accepted framework of our culture, which constructs both our questions and where our mind will rest in terms of a satisfactory answer.

So the last section will try to explain the ways in which theoretical 'paradigms' (over-arching theoretical framework affecting a number of disciplines) influence us. I will then explain the relation between explaining the world in relation to time and to space (history and anthropology). Finally I shall look at the way in which what we see is shaped by what we expect to see, particularly how we compare it to our previous experiences.

SIX

Frameworks of Understanding and Explanation

WHEN WE LOOK at any phenomenon, we come to it with a whole set of expectations and assumptions. In other words, we work within the spirit of the age, the zeitgeist, or as Kuhn has called it, a 'paradigm' or as Foucault calls it, an 'episteme' or way of knowing.

In the companion *How Do We Know*, I have explored this idea of shifting paradigms in some detail. Here I will just do two things. Firstly I will reproduce an overview of the major theoretical paradigms in the social sciences over the last half millenium, looking at some key people, attitudes to time, to power relations, the metaphors, questions and models behind the paradigm, their value and the wider world context in which they grew up. This concentrated map is expanded in a set of lectures, for which the map was produced, which explain what each means [see: 8 lectures on history of social sciences – http://upload.sms.cam.ac.uk/collection/1403004].

Secondly, I shall just look at one of the paradigms, perhaps the most important in the development of the social sciences in the twentieth century, namely *functionalism*. It is the underpinning of much of the best sociology, anthropology and history of the past hundred years and though it has some draw-backs, it is worth understanding as one way to look at our materials.

THE TEN MAJOR PARADIGMS IN WESTERN SOCIAL SCIENCE

	Circular to 1720	Progressive c.1720-1790	Pessimism c.1790-1840	Evolutionary c.1790-1840	Diffusionist c.1890-1920
People	Plato Ibn Khaldun Medieval Scholastics	Montesquieu Turgot Ferguson Adam Smith	Malthus Tocqueville (Maine) Romantic Movement	Darwin Marx & Engels Spencer Morgan Tylor Avebury	Haddon Perry Rivers (late) Elliot Smith (Frazer)
Time	Eternal return Time as a wheel Circular	Progressive growth Stages of progress Non-reversible time	Only short- term progress Dangers and traps Long-term cycles	Long-term evolution and growth Time stretches out over mil- lions of years	Long-term ripples of time spreading out through cultures
Power	The 'west' on the defensive Equality of nations	Military and productive technology of the west superior. Early Imperialism	French revolu- tion and Euro- pean division Horrors of industrial and urban revolutions Diffuse imperialism	The 'west' almost entirely dominant in every way Mature imperialism	The 'rest' catching up with the 'west' in tech- nologies and wealth Modified imperialism
Metaphor	Natural cycles Seasons Plants and animals Celestial bodies	From dark to light (enlighten- ment) From rough to smooth Simple to complex	Natural cycles Birth to death Historical cycles	Organic From seed to plant Division Diversification Complexity	Ripples in water Spread of species
Question	The meaning of life How to survive The most ideal state	What are the stages of growth? How can one improve life on earth?	How avoid the dangers ahead? Economic, demographic and political dangers	Origins of humans Placing civilizations on ladders Dynamics of evolution Homogeneity	Where have things originated? How do ideas and techniques spread?

HOW TO STUDY THE WORLD

Model	Theology History	Newtonian science Mathematics and other sciences Craft disciplines	Theology Biology	Biology Archaeology	Biology Technology
Value today	Basic categories and distinctions and ideal types	Basic types and stages of civilizations Comparative approach	Balance of optimism and pessimism Basic dangers and traps	Comparative approach Meta-histories and general laws of evolution	Relativism Connecting peoples Long-term perspective
	Agrarian civilizations	Scientific and technological growth; exploration	French revolution Urbanism and industry	Imperial dominance of the west; mature industrialism	Growth of power of Japan, India etc. First world war

	Functionalism c.1920-50	Structural Functionalism c.1935-80	Marxism c.1950-1989	Structuralism c.1940-90	Global c.1985-
People	Malinowski Richards Mair	Radcliffe-Brown Fortes Evans-Pritchard Firth Beattie Barnes Gluckman	Godelier Bloch Worsley Wolf Friedman	Levi-Strauss Leach Douglas (Mauss)	Said Marcus & Fisher Geertz (late) Goody (late) Latour
Time	Largely static Short-term change Equilibrium Cross-sectional	Static Short-term change Self-correcting equilibria, but some interest in history	Long-term evolution of systems over time Stages through which societies move	Static Layers of time	Less interest in time Political time
Power	Independence movements Two world wars and chaos of 'west' Colonialism and holding onto empire	End of colonialism and movement into post-colonialism Start of Cold War	Cold War Development and underdevelopment	Growth equality and homogeneity of technologies Striving for all kinds of equality	Global world Communicationinterdependent American hegemony

Metaphor	Complex machines with moving parts Functioning parts of a whole structure	Machines, structures of various kinds	Biological growth of animals and plants through stages	Geological strata Linguistic structuralism Binary computers	Texts and meta-texts Discourse analysis Linguistics
Question	What are the functions of a part? What is a whole? structure composed of Functions compared	How do social structures work? What is the pattern within given societies?	What is the basic determinant in history? What are the mystifications of ideology?	Relations of relations Deeper universals of the human mind Codes and thought	How does our context shape our enquiries? How can one represent the other?
Model	Biology Technology	Technology Sociology Law	Sociology History Economics	Linguistics Cybernetics and computer science Semiotics Geology	Literary analysis Media studies Aesthetics
Value	Relativism and attack on ethnocentric assumptions Ethnographic intensity of detail	Intensive studies of particular studies Deeper understanding of societies	Return to large questions and longer time spans De-mystification	Encompassing approach Affinities between levels Universals	De-privileging of the author Suspicion of hidden meta-narratives Reflexivity
	1st World War	Late Colonialism	Cold War	Digital Age	Global Age

FUNCTIONALISM

Let me now look at just one of the nine paradigms listed above in more detail.

What is functionalism? This is fairly easily answered for it is explained in the word itself. It is a philosophical theory which is based on the idea that the reason for the existence of a phenomenon, it's 'meaning,' can principally or wholly be explained by its 'function,' that is by what it does in the society where it exists and for the people who keep it going.

Choose something you want to understand and it will help to explain it: witchcraft, magic, totemism, myths, polygamy, bride burning, foot binding, the exchange of valuables, the stock exchange, public schools, the jury system. Whatever it is, in whatever society, the question to ask is 'what is its function?' By function we mean both the surface use, the manifest function, what the people say when you ask them why they are doing something, and also the deeper, latent, function, what, in the investigator's eyes, it is really doing at a more subtle level to help maintain and continue the individual, the group or the society's existence.

Functionalism is based on an analogy with a machine or any other inter-acting system which has various interrelated parts. For example the function of the brakes on a bicycle is to slow it down, the wheel's function to allow its movement over a surface, the seat is for sitting on. None of these parts can exist on their own, so functionalism conceives of a set of interconnected parts, dependent on each other, a social structure of some kind. It tends to assume that if something is present it is not just a random accident, but serves (a probably useful to the people) purpose.

This is what functionalism is, but what are its advantages and disadvantages for us? It is difficult to overstate its liberating effect when it emerged as the dominant paradigm in the early 20th century. It helped thinkers to escape from what were clearly the traps of a stage theory (Evolutionism) through which societies had to go. It made it possible to work in societies where there was no documented history, which would have been very difficult within an Evolutionary or Diffusionist framework. It undermined something of the Victorian moralizing and superiority. Phenomena like witchcraft, or arranged marriage, or shell money could be studied seriously in themselves, without needing to categorize them as primitive, irrational, backward. It encouraged moral relativism and intelligent interest in other worlds.

A second benefit was that it made it possible to compare societies more easily and also to question one's own deeper assumptions. The function of witchcraft and astrology was similar to Western psychiatry, or early barter to the stock exchange. The function of feud was similar to certain aspects of modern warfare, or the function of boys dormitories in India strongly overlapped with the function of British boarding schools.

So functionalism allows us to compare, to question our own hidden assumptions and also to stress the interconnectedness, the 'holism,' of societies. The function could only be explained by the context, by placing an institution within the rest of the system. The function of something which we might slot in as political, to do with violence and war, such as headhunting amongst the Nagas or Iban, was in fact mainly religious – a sacrificial ritual to gain the spiritual power of the head, and also a social rite of passage for young men to put themselves in a position where they could marry. In the same way, many things in our own society which look as if they are one thing, for example football as a game, are, as social scientists pointed out, also political and religious.

Yet functionalism is philosophically flawed as a theory if it is taken to an extreme, for it is patently obvious that some things have little function, but are just kept for other reasons (I see them all around me in Cambridge). Similarly, to argue that they have a function is often to deal with a tautology. If they exist, they must still have some function, even if it has changed and the strange practices are only there to attract tourists or out of a sentimental desire not to abandon them.

Ernest Gellner points out that while functionalism may be philosophically shaky, yet a potentially faulty theory has ironically led to much of the most important work in the social sciences. 'A true and important background idea (evolution) inspired faulty method and much error; and an untrue or at best half-true theory (pervasive stability, irrelevance of the past, harmonious interdependence, and mutual support of institutions) lead to valuable, accurate and illuminating research.' Gellner's explanation for this is that "the functionalist vision, however untrue in the long run and in the abstract, does greatly sharpen the observer's eye for the way in which diverse coexisting institutions set limits for each other and form some kind of more or less persisting unity. If you start your observations with functionalism as a baseline, it is not too hard to put in the corrections later, as you proceed..."[1]

The fallacy needs to be recognised particularly because, when taken to an extreme, it can have a harmful effect. The earlier argument of various writers, that we cannot know the history of small oral cultures and therefore we should concentrate on what we can know, in other words what we see and hear in a year or two of fieldwork, is reasonable. But it is easy to slip into arguing that this partial picture, with the past left out, is enough to explain things as they are, that the past is not

---

[1] GELLNER, introduction to EVANS-PRITCHARD, *A History of Anthropological Thought* (1981), p. xxii.

important and even if we could learn it about it, we should not bother with history.

The anti-historical turn was sometimes taken to an extreme. We now know that when trying to understand a phenomenon we need to know both what its function is today, why people say they believe in God or revere the Queen or go to mass or use banks, but also we would not understand any of these things without knowing something of the past history of such institutions.

* * *

When we are faced with understanding others and, in a mirror, understanding ourselves, then we need many different methodologies. It is extraordinarily difficult to enter an entirely different thought system with which we have no previous acquaintance. To believe that what at first sight may seem strange and bizarre has a function, is an enormous help. It is a leap of faith without which we could not get started.

It also alerts us to the fact that things have multiple and non-exclusive functions. Education is not just about learning facts, a dinner in an Oxbridge College is not just about eating and drinking. The more interesting functions are hidden both to the people themselves and to the observer. The knowledge that they are there, that the clues must be assembled and the underlying plot revealed, makes social science exciting and rewarding.

SEVEN

Time and Space

Are there 'laws' in history and the social sciences?

THERE HAS ALWAYS been a tension within both history and the social sciences as to whether they are arts - descriptive, evaluative, interpretative - or whether they also have something of a scientific status, the ability to generate 'laws' which can be used to establish, from particular 'experiments,' some deeper principles which apply universally.

It could well be argued that we can learn nothing durable from the study of either discipline which can be applied outside the particular context of time and space of our studies. This seems deeply disappointing. Why did I spend years investigating seventeenth-century English witchcraft cases or shamanism in a Himalayan village if I could not learn something more universal, some law, ideally of the form that 'if A and B and C exist then there will be D'?

Yet while it may seem a sad waste of time, most of those who have thought deeply have concluded that in neither of these disciplines are there laws, necessary connections. We cannot predict that people who are starving will necessarily eat or not eat their children or that people living in crowded preindustrial cities will necessarily suffer from dysentery or not do so. There are just too many factors involved. So it would appear that all we can do is paint pictures, acting like novelists or poets.

Yet there is evidence that while there are not 'laws,' there are stronger or weaker *tendencies*. This is encapsulated in Lord Acton's famous dictum that 'All power tends to corrupt. Absolute power corrupts absolutely.' All power does not necessarily and always corrupt – until it becomes all-encompassing. Yet, all else being equal, power will corrupt. Or again, in Thomas Malthus's re-formulation of his 'law of population,' population will *tend* to grow faster than resources, unless other artificial things intervene such as contraception or scientific production of food.

So we find that we can learn about tendencies, and it is these tendencies – to love, hate, friendship, playfulness, ritualistic behaviour – which I have distilled out of a life of work as a historian and anthropologist and tried to pass on to my grand-daughter in *Letters to Lily: On How the World Works* (2005).

Another way of putting this is in Mark Twain's observation that 'history does not repeat itself, but it rhymes.' Thus the McCarthy anti-communist trials of 1950s America, or exaggerated fears of terrorism today, are not the same as the anti-witchcraft trials or the persecution of the Jews in the middle ages, but they rhyme, as Arthur Miller noted in *The Crucible*.

The same is true of important sociological work, where the shape of rituals in some remote tribe in Australia gives us insight by a parallel 'rhyming' with the shape of the great rituals of advanced industrial countries, as in the Nuremberg Rallies of the Nazi period in Germany. We discover that the endless mechanism of the blood feud in Albania or among the Nagas of Assam before the arrival of the state, sheds light on the unending cycles of violence of contemporary international lawlessness in a world with no overarching government.

So in terms of the degree to which the social sciences and

history help us to understand ourselves and our world, and to make limited predictions about the future, there is little to differentiate them. We can learn from both, but cannot depend entirely on either.

CAUSES IN TIME AND SPACE

An apparent difference between historical and sociological disciplines is that the historian deals with time, being concerned with placing his information into a temporal order, while the social scientist deals with space, comparing different societies across the world. This is indeed a difference and a historian is tempted to let his or her mind rest in terms of explanation if it can be shown that something has been preceded by something else and hence that A and perhaps B and C have 'caused' D.

The social scientist feels that if we can find a set of contextually related facts, then they have 'caused' the phenomenon. So if he does some cross-comparison and finds that animal herders outside strong states have feuding societies, a great deal of small-scale violence to protect their flocks, and that this is related to male domination and tracing one's ancestors through males alone, these phenomena - which he notes across the wide sweep from North Africa to Mongolia - seem to be causally linked.

Unfortunately, as with all tendencies, it is only a matter of probabilities for we can always find exceptions. For example the Gurungs of Nepal, traditionally animal herders, had long ceased to be internally violent. Ernest Gellner believed that this was because they had exported their surplus youth and violence into the British Army. But the presence of Buddhism rather than Islam obviously complicates any easy association in this case.

In like manner it is always easy to find with historical explanations - for example the discussions of the causes of the English Civil War which used to focus on the 'Rise of the Gentry,' or of the causes of the French Revolution, with the received view that it arose out of rural poverty - that it is not as simple as that. Cause and effect are immensely complicated; all that we can hope to do is to suggest patterns, probabilities and tendencies across time and space.

INDIVIDUAL AND STRUCTURE: CHANCE AND INEVITABILITY

One of the most difficult philosophical dilemmas in both the social sciences and history is the relative role of the individual and the wider social structure. To what extent are the major changes and events in societies caused by generalized configurations of the geography, economy, social structure, ideology and political systems on the one hand and the peculiar and chance play of particular personalities on the other?

This is a topic which it is difficult for a social scientist, during a year's fieldwork, to throw much light on. A number of anthropology books and films focus on the power of a particular Big Man or prophet in swaying his people. But without much time depth and breadth of information it is difficult to go further. It is usually impossible to assess the long-term features which led to the events witnessed in the field or what happened ten or twenty years later.

Historians can often do this. The way in which the world would be different without Confucius, Alexander the Great, Newton, Napoleon or Chairman Mao has constantly intrigued historians. They have often come up with a compromise, acknowledging that the great individual is both thrown up by a type of civilization and could do nothing without it, and yet the smallest of personal accidents, the 'shape of Cleopatra's nose,' is equally important.

Certainly from my own experience working in a remote village in Nepal I could see how even there, the force of character of one or two uneducated villagers (men and women) was remarkable, and how in moments of crisis or choices the chance presence or absence of a single individual could set a village and perhaps a society flowing in a different direction.

This is all part of the wider philosophical debate as to whether chance or predestination controls societies. There is no resolution to this other than to state the obvious, namely that in both anthropology and history, before the event there are millions of possible moves, as in chess, and that life is ruled by chance. After the event, given all that has occurred before the outcome, there was only one possible way in which all the converging forces could go. As in a football game, you can't foresee the goal until it is scored. Yet once the ball is in the net it looks inevitable.

The richness of combining the social sciences and history is that it is possible to examine these complex philosophical problems with a much stronger set of tools. We can look at the movement through time and space, the macro and the micro levels, the individual and the collective, the comparative and the singular case. If we are really interested in understanding what we are and what we can do, it would be foolish not to use all the types of information and all the methods available to us.

ALAN MACFARLANE

HOW DO SOCIAL SCIENTISTS AND HISTORIANS CONSTRUCT THEIR DATA?

It was once believed that both historians and social scientists were like cameras. Many accepted the definition put forward by Samuel Johnson that the historian 'has facts ready to his hand, so he has no exercise of invention. Imagination is not required in any high degree.'[1] This is nonsense, but the recognition of its inaccuracy is not yet universal.

Likewise some early social scientists believed that one just went to a place other than one's home area, watched and listened, and wrote down what one saw or heard. 'Facts' came to one, or were captured. Social scientists were butterfly collectors, just as historians were simple-minded diggers up of old paper.

Increasingly both disciplines have realised that this is far too simple. In fact, the moment a historian selects a single piece of information and ignores others, he is bringing to the task a judgment based on a huge armoury of preconceptions and assumptions of which he cannot possibly be aware.

No piece of writing or physical object surviving from the past has any intrinsic content – it is the spectacles of our questions, assumptions and experiences that give it its meaning. Furthermore, as Marc Bloch[2] stressed, we have to 'torture' what we find to extract its meaning – we have to assume its guilt until, by cross-checking with other types of evidence bearing on the same subject, we can be sure it is to a large extent true: a real 'fact.' Our vigilance is necessary because everything that has

---

[1] BOSWELL, JAMES, *London Journal 1762-1763*. London: Heinemann, 1950, p. 293.
[2] BLOCH, MARC, *The Historian's Craft*. London: Vintage, 1954.

been said, written or made in the past was caught up in the flow of power: was part of a communication within a context.

While there is a tendency to trust inscribed documents and artefacts from the past and it takes more of an effort to be suspicious of them, it is more obvious that the social scientist constructs his or her own data and hence there is a higher degree of subjectivity in all such work. People answer questions, and answer in different ways depending on the phrasing of the question, the context, and the relationship to the asker.

THE HISTORICAL AND SOCIAL SCIENTIFIC IMAGINATION

On the whole the historian is more a prisoner of his or her information. If people in the past failed to record something, it cannot be generated two hundred years later – except occasionally by hunches and intuitions leading to the discovery of new materials.

Yet social scientists can, within limits, probe where they like and generate their own data. So anthropology often feels richer — we see the faces, hear the voices, smell the smells, all of which have gone from the parish registers, court rolls and even the diaries left to us from the past. This means that history requires more imagination in order to fill out the scribble on the page or the shape of a building.

Anthropology requires another kind of imagination in that the gap between the observer and the object of observation is often greater; although it is also true that sometimes the 'past is a foreign country.' On the whole, however, most historians tend to work within their own civilization, if not country, and to share many basic premises with their subjects. A historian of Tudor England, for example, lives within the same language, law, social system, and religion as his or her subjects.

Characteristically by contrast, anthropologists often work in societies where there is very little overlap between their own life experience and that of their subjects. Philippe Descola in his work among the Achuar Indians of the Amazonian rain forest, gives a deep insight, though he had almost nothing in common with the ideas of time and space, person, identity, nature and culture and morality of these almost entirely different peoples. Anthropology in this view appears impossible.

Yet the magic of anthropology in the hands of its best exponents lies in its ability to cross over to the other side, entering another world, while retaining the observer's own identity in order to maintain the strangeness, and then translate back a totally different set of assumptions into terms comprehensible to your audience. It is the art of suspending judgements and entering other worlds through sympathy and empathy.

The magic of great historians is to recreate, through a deep knowledge of a wide range of sources, and the filling in of absences through intuition, largely vanished worlds with all their richness.

* * *

Apart from the technical training and tools in both – the art of 'reading' the materials through palaeography or linguistics – and the endless curiosity and sense of exploration that are needed in both, probably the most important characteristic needed in both disciplines is self-knowledge. In both, the depth of the work reflects the degree to which the practitioner has risen above his or her self and come to look down on his or her own life, arranging his or her experiences into a complex model of how people can behave so that he or she can enter their other worlds.

THE NECESSITY OF COMBINING SPACE WITH TIME

What is certain is that in the pursuit of larger and more serious problems it is impossible to proceed far without having to join social science and history. For example, apart from the very smallest and most remote societies, we cannot understand much about the present without investigating the past, not only the more recent but also the deeper past; and likewise to understand the past we need to think about the present.

To understand Japan, England or China, which I have tried to do for many years, we need the questions from the social sciences and the materials from history. None of these civilizations can be understood by a cross-sectional study of a few years in the present. But nor can feudal Japan or England be understood without wider comparative models of power from social science. Social science without history is superficial, shallow and unconvincing. History without social science can be insular, ethnocentric and often rather trivial, asking questions that interest us now but soon will seem very dated.

What this shows is that we should remember Lord Acton's dictum – 'study problems not periods.' Problems extend beyond disciplinary boundaries. As Marc Bloch put it 'the good historian is like the giant of the fairy tale. He knows that wherever he catches the scent of human flesh, there his quarry lies.'[1] The same, of course, is true of all the social sciences. 'What social science is properly about' urged Wright-Mills, 'is the human variety, which consists of all the social worlds in which men have lived, are living, and might live.'[2]

If we study problems we will soon find that we move outside even history and the social sciences. Almost immediately we invoke all the human disciplines and perhaps some of the sciences. Thus, for example, when I was studying the history and impact of glass in world civilizations I needed to learn something about scientific instruments, ophthalmology, art history, materials science, Chinese and Islamic civilizations, and much else.

THE BLINKERS OF 'MODERNITY'

Another advantage of combining anthropology with history is that it lets us participate in several different social systems in parallel. Those who find themselves in 'modern' societies are by definition educated and live their daily existence in worlds where there has been a serious attempt to break apart the four constituents of human life – wealth, belief, society and power. So there is an attempt to act *as if* religion and politics, economics and family life, law and politics can be separated into largely autonomous institutions. Of course the divisions often fail, but we are systematically educated to separate – head and heart, God and money, family and politics.

This leads to some efficiency and liberty, but makes it less

---

[1] BLOCH, *The Historian's Craft*, p.26.
[2] WRIGHT-MILLS, C, *The Sociological Imagination*. Oxford: Oxford University Press, 1959, p.147.

easy to understand the recent past of most civilizations where the divisions work differently. We can become very tempero- or western-centric and unable to understand interconnected and holistic worlds, not only of tribes and peasantries, but even of mediaeval and early modern societies.

Anthropologists work in holistic societies, civilizations where people are deeply inter-dependent, which have not gone through these divisions, and they therefore have to suspend their divided thinking if they are to understand anything. The shock of finding something so different to their own 'scientific' and 'rational' and 'separated' world makes them see this richness and power of organic and holistic worlds. Reading their accounts, as well as our own experience, if we are fortunate enough to live for a period in such undivided or differently divided societies, extends our vision and makes it easier to understand almost all of history and most of anthropology.

EIGHT

Contrast and Compare

A NY HISTORIAN OR social scientist will be aware that all the time s/he is indulging in comparison. In the case of history, the comparisons are usually in time, in social science, predominantly in space. The most familiar method of the historian is to take his or her own society as the norm, and then to see how far the past is similar or different from this. This is also what an anthropologist tends to do, taking his or her own society as the yardstick against which to measure things.

This comparison of one's own present society with either the past of the same country or with another is a perfectly reasonable procedure, and all I am suggesting here is that the method be made a little more explicit.

Alexis de Tocqueville's work illustrates the method of comparison being used explicitly, though the results are concealed. 'In my work on America ... Though I seldom mentioned France, I did not write a page without thinking of her, and placing her as it were before me. And what I especially tried to draw out, and to explain in the United States, was not the whole condition of that foreign society, but the points in which it differs from our own, or resembles us. It is always by noticing likenesses or contrasts that I succeeded in giving an interesting and accurate description....'[1]

The necessity of comparison is well stressed by Evans-Pritchard: 'in the widest sense there is no other method. Comparison is, of course, one of the essential procedures of all sciences and one of the elementary processes of human thought.'[2]

DISTANCING THE OVER-FAMILIAR

A first use of the comparative method is to act like a reverse telescope, pushing away things which are too close, so that a gap is created and one can see them. This might be termed, 'distancing the (over) familiar,' or turning the obvious into the unobvious.

One difficulty for all analysts is the strong pressure to leave unquestioned (and hence unexplained) a great deal of behaviour in the past or in other societies because it is similar to our own and hence selfevidently 'normal.' As David Hume wrote, 'the views the most familiar to us are apt, for that very reason, to escape us' or as Braudel put it, '... surprise and distance... are both equally necessary for an understanding of that which surrounds you   surrounds you so evidently that you can no longer see it clearly.'[3]

Likewise, as Marx wrote 'Human history is like palaeontology. Owing to a certain judicial blindness even the best intelligences absolutely fail to see the things which lie in front of

---

[1] DE TOCQUEVILLE, *Memoir I*, p.1,359.
[2] EVANS-PRITCHARD, E.E., *The Comparative Method in Social Anthropology* (1963) p.3.
[3] D.HUME quoted in DUMONT, MANDEVILLE, 19; BRAUDEL in ed. *Burke, Economy and Society*, p.24.

their noses...'[1] This was understood two and a half thousand years ago by Confucius. 'As the fish swims in the water but is unmindful of the water, the bird flies in the wind but knows not of the wind.'[2]

The problem is acute for the historian of his own culture who needs some 'external fulcrum' in order even to be able to be aware of the central features of the past. Such a fulcrum is automatically present for an anthropologist who works in an alien culture, but even he needs support for, as Homans argued, 'when a man describes a society which is not his own, he often leaves out those features which the society has in common with his own society.'[3]

The benefits of a wider knowledge of alternative social structures through the comparative method acts as a distancer of the familiar parts of the past. This is probably what Bloch was referring to when he wrote that 'The comparative method in the hand of ethnographers has restored to us with a kind of mental shock this sense of the difference, the exotic element, which is the indispensable condition for a balanced understanding of the past.'[4] For, as he wrote elsewhere, 'to speak of discovery is also to speak of surprise and dissimilarity.'[5]

FAMILIARISING THE DISTANT

Equally problematic is the fact that many things are so unfamiliar and distant that we cannot get inside their logic or 'understand'

---

[1] MARX, KARL, *Pre-Capitalist Economic Formations*, ed. E.J. HOBSBAWM (1964), p.140.
[2] KOESTLER, ARTHUR, *The Lotus and the Robot* (1960), p.269.
[3] HOMANS, G.C., *English Villagers of the Thirteenth Century* (1960), p.382.
[4] BLOCH, MARC, *Land and Work in Medieval Europe* (1967), p.47.
[5] BLOCH, MARC, *The Historian's Craft*. London: Vintage (1954), p.120.

them. Since, according to R. G. Collingwood, the historian has to imaginatively re-create the past in his own mind, any helps to this process are welcome. In this difficulty, we need to use the method with the telescope in its normal position, in other words to bring the phenomena closer. This is a particular problem for anthropologists, but it also afflicts historians.

Often the historian of longdistant times or of social groups of which he is not a member, finds himself regarding a world which is based on premises so alien to his own that he cannot understand it at all. For instance, Collingwood argued in relation to Roman religion that 'though we have no lack of data about Roman religion, our own religious experience is not of such a kind as to qualify us for reconstructing in our own minds what it meant to them.'[1]

The difficulty was well described by David Hume: 'Let an object be presented to a man of never so strong natural reason and abilities; if that object be entirely new to him, he will not be able, by the most accurate examination of its sensible qualities, to discover any of its causes or effects.'[2] The usual temptation is either to avoid the subject altogether, or to dismiss it as irrational nonsense.

How does the comparative approach help? One way is through providing hypotheses concerning how some utterly strange system may work. This may be related to one of the two methods which the mathematician Polya suggests are used to solve complex problems[2]: "ransack our memory for any similar problem of which the solution is known."[3]

---
1 COLLINGWOOD, R.G, *The Idea of History*. Oxford: Oxford University Press, 1946, p.329.
2 WINCH, P, *The Idea of a Social Science*. London, Routledge, 1958, p.7.
3 BURGESS, ROBERT G. (ed.), *Field Research: A Sourcebook and Field Manual* (1982), p.217.

Now the solution may be 'known' in a sort of way through the studies of others in other societies. Examples would be the insights which anthropological studies of curious phenomena like the blood feud or witchcraft gave to historians studying the same phenomena in the West.

The comparative method provides possible alternative models of how things might be connected and what they might mean, it brings them within our range of comprehension, hence partly overcoming Hume's problem.

MAKING THE ABSENCES VISIBLE

A third important service the comparative method can provide is by revealing absences. In all societies, many of the most interesting things are the absences, and it is extremely difficult to notice these. What I mean is rather well illustrated by Robert Smith, who recounts how a Japanese scholar who was asked why ancestor worship persists in modern Japan said 'That is not an interesting question. The real question is why it died out in the West.'[1] Of course, both are interesting questions but the absence is certainly just as curious.

For instance, many of the most important features in Japan and England are the absences – the dogs that did not bark in the night – the weakness of kinship, the anti-intolerance of religion, the non-authoritarian balance of the State. These can only be detected if we have a strong positive image of what is 'normal' in the course of history, and then see that in the special cases the predicted did not happen – and something strange did.

---

[1] SMITH, ROBERT J., *Japanese Society* (1983), p.152.

TESTING ANSWERS

Another use for the comparative tool is through its ability to test simple hypotheses. Although historians are aware that they are not trying to establish general laws, their 'descriptions' always contain elements of causal connections of the form 'If this, then that.' They are constantly on the lookout for both necessary and sufficient causes, links of a specific and general kind. In this task, they can and probably must, use comparisons. If they start with a problem such as 'What caused the English Civil War,' 'What were the effects of printing' or 'What caused the industrial revolution,' they are always seeking causal connections and co-variations. Having come up with some hypothesis, they nearly always need to move outside the particular instance to see if the connection holds more widely. For instance, if Calvinism is thought to be a necessary cause of 'Capitalism,' are there 'Capitalist' societies that are not 'Calvinist'?

Thus, as Nadel writes, 'Even if we are initially concerned only with a single society and the appearance in it of a particular social fact (which we wish to 'explain'), our search of covariations capable of illuminating our problem will often lead us beyond that society to others, similar or diverse, since the given society may not offer an adequate range of variations.'[1]

It may be that historians will claim that they are not trying to make general statements, but any brief look into their work shows that they usually are. Any general statement has to be tested cross-comparatively. 'It is also evident that if any general statements are to be made about social institutions they can only

---

[1] NADEL, *Foundations*, p.227.

be made by comparison between the same type of institutions in a wide range of societies.'[1]

METHODS OF COMPARISON

Comparison can be undertaken in numerous ways, each appropriate to its task, and we cannot lay down in advance which would be the most appropriate. All we can do is to raise some of the alternatives facing us when undertaking comparisons.

One of the first things to think about is whether we are principally interested in locating similarities or differences between those things compared – though, in fact we have to do both.

Evans-Pritchard writes that 'I would like to place emphasis on the importance for social anthropology, as a comparative discipline, of differences, because it could be held that in the past the tendency has often been to place the stress on similarities...whereas it is the differences which would seem to invite sociological explanation. This is an involved question, for institutions have to be similar in some respects before they can be different in others...'[2]

Others have written similarly. Marc Bloch wrote 'there is no true understanding without a certain range of comparison; provided, of course, that comparison is based upon differing and, at the same time, related realities.'[3] The idea of similarity with difference is elaborated by Nadel. The comparative approach 'means, in essence, the analysis of social situations which are at first sight already comparable, that is, which appear to share

---

1 EVANS-PRITCHARD, E.E., *The Comparative Method in Social Anthropology* (1963), p.3.
2 EVANS-PRITCHARD, *Comparative*, p.17.
3 BLOCH, *Craft*, p.42.

certain features (modes of action, relationships) while differing in others, or to share their common features with some degree of difference."[1]

UNITS OF COMPARISON

The success of the comparative method will, of course, heavily depend on the comparison of things that can be compared. This consists of several features. One is that the units compared are roughly of the same order of magnitude – for instance, it would clearly be foolish to compare the handshake in England with the family system in China.

Secondly, in order for comparison to be effective, there must be some common ground, as well as difference. Things must be of the same class or order in some way. Thus to compare, say, marriage in America with tea chewing in China would probably be fruitless. The selection of the comparisons is all important and is usually deceptive since words like 'city,' 'marriage,' 'family' etc. are notoriously slippery and difficult to compare.

This is perhaps why anthropologists have tended to shy away from comparing 'things' in themselves, and stress the need to compare relationships. "The comparison can only be conducted in terms of relations, and not of items or isolated institutions; and this relational comparison begins from the moment that the research worker approaches his material."[2]

They have also reacted against the tendency to wrench bits of culture out of their context and stress the need to compare a whole culture, e.g. need to compare whole social systems "a

---

[1] NADEL, *Foundations*, p.222.
[2] POCOCK, D., *Social Anthropology* (1961), p.114.

solid and thorough comparison of values is possible only between two systems taken as wholes...'[1]

CONTRAST AND COMPARE

We also need to distinguish contrast (A is different from B in the following...), and comparison (A and B have certain features in common and certain differences). Both have their place. The contrast method can stimulate thought. As Wright Mills puts it, advocating the studying of extremes and opposites. 'Often you get the best insights by considering extremes by thinking of the opposite of that with which you are directly concerned. If you think about despair, then also think about elation; if you study the miser, then also the spendthrift.'[2] Or again, he writes, that in order to stimulate mental activity, "...what you can do is to give the range and the major types of some phenomenon, and for that it is more economical to begin by constructing 'polar types,' opposites along various dimensions."[3]

While the method of contrast is initially stimulating, in the long run it is probably not as fruitful as that of comparison. It helps with posing questions; for instance the contrast method might lead one to ask why English and Japanese cities do not usually have walls, why neither country had 'castes,' why neither had developed concepts of pollution, why there were no professional money-lenders in the villages of seventeenth century England. But while stimulating questions, it gives little help in suggesting answers.

---

[1] DUMONT, LOUIS, *Essays on Individualism, Modern Ideology in Anthropological Perspective* (1986), p.243.
[2] WRIGHT-MILLS, Sociological, p.235
[3] WRIGHT-MILLS, Sociological, p.235

HOW MANY POLES OF COMPARISON?

Usually, when just two types are brought into play, for instance 'holism' and 'individualism,' or 'hot' and 'cold' or 'pre-industrial' and 'industrial,' then one is dealing with contrasts. As stated above, this is a start, but only a start.

Much more fruitful are three-way comparisons, or even, as I am currently attempting, five-way comparisons between China, Japan, Islam, Europe and the Anglo-sphere. Then it becomes possible to look at variables where there are similarities between two of the examples, but a variation in the others. Some of the most fruitful applications of the method have had three poles of comparison, for instance De Tocqueville with England, America and France, or Norman Jacobs with China, Japan and Europe. And much of Max Weber's work drew its strength because he was interested in Europe, India and China.

Afterword

Books on intellectual methods tend to be worthy, but dull. Like gardening manuals when set against the experience of gardening, cookery books when compared to the pleasures of cooking and eating, or fishing guides, when we compare them to the joys of the rod in the hand, they pale into the prosaic when compared to the experience we are trying to introduce. Yet there is a need for the manuals as a start. Many gardens, meals and rivers would be less exciting without the advice given in a manual.

As explained at the start, I was expected to learn by doing. Very little formal instruction was given to me about how to find out about the various worlds I have explored. I think I would have been the better off for a book such as this, even though it is really only when we try, and often fail, that we begin to appreciate help. I think that we do gain experience in our lives, and though each of our lives is different, something can be passed on, as I have tried to pass on over half a century of experience to you.

It is in this hope that I have written various accounts in a number of small books on 'How the World Works' and how we can study and learn about it. I realize that the way of understanding the world has changed immensely since I first started to try to study it at school in the 1950's. Particularly in the last twenty years, the spread of the Internet has brought many new opportunities and also challenges.

Yet as I look back over the way in which thinkers since the sixteenth century and earlier worked, and compare it to my own life in the Internet Age, I see many continuing and recurring deeper techniques and approaches that helped then and now work for me. I hope that a few of them will also make your intellectual journeys more rewarding. Perhaps one day you will write a new, updated, and much improved version of this little book. I do hope so.

Further Reading and References

INTERVIEWING

BERNARD, H. RUSSELL, *Research Methods in Anthropology*, London: Sage, (1994).
DOUGLAS, JACK D, *Creative Interviewing*, London. Sage Publications, (1985).
GOODY, JACK, *The Expansive Moment; the rise of social anthropology in Britain and Africa 1918-1970*, Cambridge: Cambridge University Press (1995).
LANGNESS, L.L, *The Life History in Anthropological Science*, New York: Holt, Rinehart and Winston (1965).

WRITING

BLOCH, MARC, *The Historian's Craft*, Manchester: Manchester University Press, (1954).
BURGESS, ROBERT G. (ED.), *Field Research: A Sourcebook and Field Manual* (1982).
CLIFFORD, JAMES., MARCUS, GEORGE., *Writing Culture: The Poetics and Politics of Ethnography*. Berkeley: Univ. of California Press (2010).
COLLINS, RANDALL, *Weberian Sociological Theory* (1986).

DE TOCQUEVILLE, ALEXIS, *Memoir, Letters, and Remains of Alexis de Tocqueville* (1861).
DUMONT, LOUIS, *Essays on Individualism, Modern Ideology in Anthropological Perspective* (1986).
EVANS-PRITCHARD, E. E, 'Some Reminiscences and Reflections on Fieldwork', *Journal of the Anthropological Society of Oxford* (1973), 4: 1-12.
GEERTZ, CLIFFORD, *Works and Lives, the Anthropologist as Author*, Stanford: Stanford University Press (1989).
GEERTZ, CLIFFORD, *After the Fact: Two countries, four decades, one anthropologist*, Harvard: Harvard University Press (1996).
GERTH, H.H. & MILLS C. WRIGHT (EDS.), *From Max Weber: Essays in Sociology* (1967).
KOESTLER, ARTHUR, *The Act of Creation* (1964).
KOESTLER, ARTHUR, *The Lotus and the Robot* (1960)
MACFARLANE, ALAN, *How to Discover the World; Reflections for Rosa*, Amazon: CreateSpace (2013).
MARCUS, GEORGE E. & FISCHER, MICHAEL, *Anthropology as Cultural Critique, an experimental movement in the human sciences*, Chicago: Chicago University Press (1986)
MAUSS, MARCEL, *The Gift, forms and functions of exchange in archaic societies*, London: Routledge and Kegan Paul (1954).
NADEL, S.F, *The Foundations of Social Anthropology* (1963).
ORWELL, GEORGE, *Politics and the English Language* (London: Penguin. *Horizon*, Penguin Modern Classics, 2013). [Originally published in *Horizon*, 1946].
POCOCK, D., *Social Anthropology* (1961).
POWDERMAKER, HORTENSE, *Stranger and Friend, The Way of an Anthropologist*. New York: Norton & Company. (1966)
RICHARDSON, ROBERT.D, *First We Read, Then We Write.*

Emerson on the Creative Process. Iowa: University of Iowa Press. (2009)
ROBBEN, ANTONIUS C.G.M AND SLUKA, JEFFREY A, EDS., *Ethnographic Fieldwork: An Anthropological Reader.* Oxford: Blackwell [part IX, 'Reflexive Ethnography'] (2007).
SRINIVAS, M.N, *The Remembered Village.* Berkeley: California University Press, (1976).
WEBB, BEATRICE, *My Apprenticeship* (1st edn., no date).
WRIGHT MILLS, C. *The Sociological Imagination.* New York: Oxford University Press, (1959).

FUNCTIONALISM AND PARADIGMS

BEATTIE, JOHN., 'Explanation in Social Anthropology: Social Function and Social Structure' in *Other Cultures* (1964).
EVANS-PRITCHARD, E.E., 'Anthropology and History,' in *Essays in Social Anthropology* (1962).
EVANS-PRITCHARD, E.E., *The Comparative Method in Social Anthropology* (1963).
MARION J. LEVY., 'Structural Functional Analysis' and FRANCESCA M. CANCIAN, 'Varieties of Functional Analysis' in *International Encyclopedia of the Social Sciences* (1968).
MALINOWSKI, BRONISLAW, *Magic, Science and Religion, and other Essays* (1954).
MACFARLANE, ALAN, 'Paradigms in the West' in *How Do We Know* (2014).
MARX, KARL, *Pre-Capitalist Economic Formations*, ed. E.J. Hobsbawm (1964)
RADCLIFFE-BROWN, A.R., *Structure and Function in Primitive Society* (1952).

TIME AND SPACE

BLOCH, MARC, *The Historian's Craft*. London: Vintage, (1954)
BLOCH, MARC, *Land and Work in Medieval Europe* (1967)
BOSWELL, JAMES, *London Journal 1762-1763*. London: Heinemann (1950).
BRAUDEL, FERNAND, *The Mediterranean World of Philip II*. London: Collins (1972).
BURCKHARDT, JACOB, *The Civilizations of the Renaissance in Italy*. London: Phaidon (1960).
BURKE, PETER, *Sociology and History*. London: George Allen and Unwin (1980).
COHN, BARNEY, *An Anthropologist among the Historians and Other Essays*. Oxford: Oxford University Press(1991).
COLLINGWOOD, R.G, *The Idea of History*. Oxford: Oxford University Press (1946).
DESCOLA, PHILIPPE, *The Spears of Twilight: Life and Death in the Amazon Jungle*. New York: Harper Collins. (1996)
ELTON, GEOFFREY, *The Practice of History*, London: Collins. (1967)
EVANS-PRITCHARD, E.E. *Essays in Social Anthropology*. London: Faber, (1962)
GOODY, JACK, *The Development of the Family and Marriage in Europe*. Cambridge: Cambridge University Press, (1983).
HOMANS, G.C., *English Villagers of the Thirteenth Century*, (1960).
LADURIE, LE ROY, *Montaillou*. London: Penguin (1980).
MACFARLANE, ALAN, *The Riddle of the Modern World*. London: Macmillan (2000).
MACFARLANE, ALAN, *Letters to Lily; On How the World Works*.

London: Profile, (2005).

MALINOWSKI, BRONISLAW, *A Diary in the Strict Sense of the Term*. New York: Harcourt Brace, (1967).

SMITH, ROBERT J., *Japanese Society* (1983).

THOMAS, KEITH, 'History and Anthropology.' *Past and Present*, vol. 24. (1963).

THOMAS, KEITH, *Religion and the Decline of Magic*. London: Weidenfeld and Nicholson (1971).

WINCH, P, *The Idea of a Social Science*. London, Routledge (1958).

WRIGHT-MILLS, C, *The Sociological Imagination*. Oxford: Oxford University Press (1959).

ALAN MACFARLANE

How We Understand the World

THIS BOOK IS part of a series of short letters written to young friends. Encouraged by the reception of my Letters to Lily (2005), I decided to write a set of letters to her younger sister – Reflections for Rosa. I was then asked by other friends to write short books for their children.

In each I try to explore some aspect of 'How We Understand the World,' based on my experience as an anthropologist and historian at Cambridge University. I have tried to put into simple words what I have learnt about discovery, creativity and methods to understand our complex world.

EXPLORE THE SERIES

1 How to Discover the World *Reflections for Rosa*
2 How to Investigate Mysteries *Secrets for Sam*
3 How to Study the World *Suggestions for Shuo*
4 How do We Know *Advice for April*
5 How to Understand Each Other *Notes for Nina*
6 The Survival Manual *Thoughts for Taras*
7 A Modern Education *Advice for Ariston*
8 Learning to be Modern *Jottings for James*
9 Intelligent Machines *Conversations with Gerry*

Image on front cover is an adaptation of Jesus and the Disciples on the Road to Emmaus by Pieter Bruegel the Elder, available in the public domain.

www.ingramcontent.com/pod-product-compliance
Lightning Source LLC
Chambersburg PA
CBHW061331040426
42444CB00011B/2874